Tripping with

Tripping with the King and Others

Salvatore R. Orefice

2007

Tripping with the King and Others

For my dear friend, Mel Frohman

CHAPTER ONE

1960

Salvatore Orefice is my name, I'm twenty-eight years old, my sun sign is Leo, my rising sign is Taurus, twice married, twice divorced, I have two sons and a daughter. I'm a barber. I've been cutting hair for fifteen years. I've owned and operated several barbershops in my prosaic career. Now, cutting hair is a dark interior I want to transcend.

I'm musing thus while sitting alongside my barber friend, Rick Mills, in his shiny TR3 Triumph sports car, parked across the street from Jay Sebring's prestigious hair salon for men. Rick is a fast-talking, gum-chomping sharpy. At the moment he's rattling on trying to convince me that we should both try and get a job at the Sebring salon.

"He's a first class act, a cosmetologist, a hairdresser, not a regular barber. The guy is making big bucks, getting famous for his revolutionary approach to cutting men's hair," says Rick.

Like I said, I'm musing. Con permiso, a quick digression, to get an idea where I'm coming from...

1940

BRONX, NEW YORK

I'm eight-years old. After school and on Saturdays, I work in my Uncle Joe's barbershop. I shine shoes, sweep up hair hair, empty spittoons and carefully clean a sparkling array of bottles—hair tonic, witch hazel, bay rum—all cool, crisp and colorful. On Saturdays when the shop is busy, my Uncle has me apply hot lather—which I vigorously rub onto the week-long stubbled faces he will expertly shave. My uncle is a genuine dapper, with polished wing-tipped shoes, mustache precisely trimmed, and always sporting a fresh rose pinned to the pocket of his starched white smock. He has three barbers working in the shop. They, too, are expert barbers, but none of them can compare with him. He's the master and they know it.

It's fascinating watching Uncle Joe shave someone. First, there's the sharp crack of the straight razor slapped onto a leather strop which hangs from the side of the huge barber chair. Then, with his feathery light forefinger, he feels the surgically-sharp edge of the razor. If it's not perfecto, it's a few more strokes until he's satisfied. Then, with his small soft hands and quick precise strokes, my uncle glides the razor over your face, moving it as if it's in a finely choreographed ballet. A few masterful strokes, zip zip, and he's done with the shaving. Then there's a couple of gentle smacks of bay rum followed by a light dusting of face powder. Finished.

Man, you have to feel good after that. Bad-asses turn into purring pussycats. All it takes is a few minutes of barber services — only with Uncle Joe it's not a service, it's a religious experience, with his shop an oasis, a place to relax and enjoy. The customers are mostly Italian-Americans, Irish and Jewish, all male, none of the unisex bullshit. It's great, men being men sans the psychosexual paranoia we have nowadays.

It's Saturday night that I most enjoy. Around nine o'clock, after closing the shop, the "Compahs" (i.e., close friends) arrive — at least a dozen men with food, wine, guitars and mandolins ready to party. It doesn't take long for the desired high to be reached. Then each hardworking stiff becomes a passionately involved musician/singer. Midway through the soiree, I'm sent to the corner tavern for a fresh bucket of brew. I hurry back to the shop (having a few swigs for myself) not wanting to miss a single moment of the fervent emotions acted out against a backdrop of tonic bottles and shaving mugs. Then I sit cross-legged on a regal barber chair, wondrous and happy, listening to the mandolins mewing into the summer night.

1942

I'm eleven years old, the Second World War is going on. I'm riding with my father, mother, sister and baby brother in a stuffy, smoky train jammed with drunken and half-drunken servicemen. Both sides of our big family are migrating to sunny California, looking for a prosperous and healthful life (my father quit his job as an elevator operator in one of those monster skyscrapers in the city). Some of us travel by train, others by car. Amidst thick layers of cigarette smoke, I solemnly sit with starched shirt, tie and knickers — my usual resplendent self.

I ruefully survey the ubiquitous war propaganda posters plastered throughout the train. One of the posters depicts Uncle Sam smashing the venomous enemy (Mussolini, Tojo and Hitler), his huge fists about to squash them like loathsome vermin. Another poster reads "A Slip Of The Lip Will Sink a Ship." I'm straining my eyes trying to see what's in the background of the poster—it's an American aircraft carrier bellowing huge columns of smoke as it slowly sinks to its watery grave. I see the venal faces of Hitler, Mussolini and Tojo relishing the scene. Why does Uncle Sam want to kill Italians? Am I the enemy? My mother assures me that I'm not the enemy and reaffirms my dignity by straightening my tie.

My father says, "You are an Italian-American. Remember that. Between your mother's side of the family and my side of the family you have eight uncles fighting in the war for the United States of America. Capish?"

I capish, but I feel really shitty about being Italian. Maybe if I scrunch my face and hold my breath I can pass for Irish, then I won't be recognized as the enemy. The enemy...I slowly settle down into the smelly train seat and gaze at the passing countryside. I'm leaving the Bronx with it's stoop-to-stoop Italians. I'm going to sunny California. I should be happy. I feel like shit.

We arrive in Los Angeles at Fifty-fourth and Broadway. We're temporarily living with my Sicilian grandparents, who came to California a few months earlier, along with two of my uncles and a teenage aunt. The very first thing I notice is a blue banner with five gold stars pinned to the front door of the house. I ask my grandfather, "What's that all about?"

"Five sons, youse uncles, fight in da war. Each a star, she's a you uncle. Capish?" says my Grandfather.

I nod yes.

"Yousa know why they inna dis a war, Sonny?" (Sonny is my nickname).

I shake my head "no" because "tutti pazi" ("everyone is nuts").

"Boom a boom. Dey shoots each other. Everybody shoots everybody. Pazo! Tutti!" My grandfather shakes his head. He's old-world Sicilian. Wiry, undershirted, ten days stubble of beard, wine and garlic breath. He acts out every scene when he talks to you. He's a super-macho man, who sings like an angel. I love him.

A week later, my first day of school, I'm dressed in my usual starched shirt, tie, knickers and shiny shoes. I'm fastidious, I like to feel neat. Scurrying along thus, I'm promptly jumped by several Pachucos (Mexican-American zootsuiters) who commence to beat the living shit out of my spiffy ass.

In spite of my really crummy welcome to Los Angeles, the place is growing on me and I'm caught-up in the whole Hollywood scene. Hey, here I am in movie-star land. At night I can hear music coming from the corner ballroom, big band, jazzy music drifting through the clement air. I lay in bed and wonder what I will be when I'm a grown man.

I'm sitting on the front steps of my grandparents' house watching a dull yellow streetcar clanking by. Plastered on the sides of the streetcar are several war propaganda posters grimly depicting the enemy—Tojo, Mussolini, Hitler—looking approvingly on as a toothy Japanese soldier is dragging off a near-naked female, his venal sneer telling us he is about to rape her. In the background, I see burning houses and dead bodies strewn across a bloody battlefield. The poster reads "Destroy The Enemy, Buy War Bonds." Behind me the screen door creaks open. "Let's a go, Sonny," says my grandfather.

"Where to?" I ask.

"Fort Ross," drawls my cousin Sammy Boy. He's twenty years old, a street savvy character who doesn't take himself too seriously (he's deferred from the draft because of a perforated eardrum). We climb into the front seat of Sammy Boy's meticulously polished pickup truck, complete with furry foxtails on the radio antenna, and shove off.

"So Fort Ross?" I ask.

"It's where we get the soldiers."

"Soldiers?"

"Yeah, soldiers. Italian prisoners of war."

"Italians"?

"What'd I say? Yeah, wops, dagos."

"The enemy?" I respond incredulously.

"Yeah the enemy. But right now a few of the enemy are gonna be staying with us for the weekend."

I don't say a word. I'm staring out the window. Heavy confusion... This is a complicated world. I'm learning. Now Sammy Boy laughs as he makes a sharp turn and we lean into each other, tight, like a family.

An hour later we arrive at Fort Ross. Guards, gates, fences, guns. After they check us out, we're permitted to enter the prison grounds. It's certainly not what I thought a prison would be, what with manicured lawns, beds of colorful flowers, fish ponds and pebbled pathways, which a few prisoners (wearing American uniforms with shoulder patches reading "Italia") are diligently attending. We make a few wrong turns, and I see rows of pasta drying on clotheslines behind a mess hall. A couple of more wrong turns, then I'm inhaling the mouth-watering aroma of pasta sauce cooking.

I face Sammy Boy. "This is a prison camp? It's unbelievable," I dubiously utter.

"This is something, eh?" says Sammy Boy as he points to a couple of prisoners sitting on the steps of a barracks. One of the prisoners is peeling potatoes while the other strums a guitar.

"Dey look a like a nice boys," says my grandfather.

"The place is a country club," pipes Sammy Boy.

"Good a boys," mumbles my grandfather.

A few more cryptic turns and we finally reach our destination, a ubiquitous barrack, in front of which our weekend guests anxiously await our arrival. Six of them, in their teens and early twenties, friendly, good-humored. They thank us profusely for our kindness as they pile onto the truck bed. One of them looks a couple of years older than me. He gives me a thin, timorous smile. "Bon giorno," he says.

"Bon giorno," I reply. "Welcome to America," I blurt, feeling like a jerk. I mean, he's still a prisoner of war, the enemy and all.

Later on at our house that evening, after consuming heroic amounts of food and wine, the POW's loosen up and talk about the war in North Africa. I'm hanging on to every syllable. It seems the Germans forced the Italian troops to go in front of them so that they would receive the brunt of the action.

"Couldn't you run away," asks my father.

"The Germans, dey shoot us if we run a back. If we run in a front, the Americanos, dey shoot a us!" pops the kid that looks a couple of years older than me.

"We go dis away, boom boom. We go that a way, boom boom," adds another prisoner.

"So, what the hell did ya do?" asks Sammy Boy.

All the prisoners turn to the one they call Capitano (although no ranking insignias are visible), who looks about twenty years old. He pours himself a hefty glass of vino, downs it in one gulp, then slowly stands and faces us.

"As soon as we get out of the range of the German guns, we throw down our guns and we run like hell to the American lines, waving a big white sheet that you can see for miles away," says the Capitano in perfect English.

"We surrender!" shouts the kid prisoner.

Then silence, and within the silence there is clarity. The prisoners look at each other, no explanations, it's a matter of pain remembered...

In concert, they thank us profusely with tears of gratitude for the Americans that got them to the safety of a prison camp.

That's how it goes for the next few months. The prisoners stay at our house on weekends. The guys are becoming part of our family. Singing, dancing, having a hell of a good time. I look forward to the weekends.

Now get this. My Uncle Tony, a soldier, who is diligently killing Italians in North Africa—for which he's been heavily decorated—unexpectedly shows up at our front door. His forehead is bandaged, one arm in a sling, he's leaning on a cane—what does he see? The enemy. Singing, dancing, having a hell of a good time. The look on his face is a cold animal stare, his beat-up body sinking deeper into his cane. He lowers his head and sighs deeply, accepting the riveting reality.

A few weeks after my Uncle Tony's untimely arrival, my grandfather dies. I feel, rather, I know, the "Italian thing" is gone. The old world... Gone forever. I'll miss him, truly miss him.

Several months later my folks buy a small house in Burbank and we move to the suburbs. Fresh air, scenic surrounding mountains, wide-open blue sky—which unfortunately darkens when squadrons of war planes drone over my callow head, folks cheering them on, "Kill the Japs, Germans, Wops!" Makes me feel real good, the "Kill the Wops" part.

The Lockheed Aircraft factory is about a mile away from our house. I get a summer job washing dishes at the Y.P. 38 Cafe. I'm twelve. The cafe is about half as big as a small closet, a peeling pile of rubble, complete with a boozer cook and a big-titted waitress who walks and talks like John Wayne. Every other day the cook passes out in the can. Now I'm forced to do the cooking. I don't know shit about cooking, however, it didn't take long to learn. Simple gringo stuff—mashed potatoes, lima beans, Salisbury steak. Like I said, gringo fare.

When the noonday siren wails, a voracious mob descends onto the joint like a berserk swarm of locusts, cleaning the place out right down to the last onion. Now a really shitty thing happens. I'm facing a whopping pile of dirty dishes to be washed. After a few months of wrinkled hands, I quit.

I'm into comic books and I know the delivery date for every drugstore in town. My room is methodically stacked from floor to ceiling with comic books. "The Green Lantern," "Captain Marvel," "Captain America," "Terry and The Pirates," "Smiling Jack"...the list goes on. I stay in my room for hours on end absorbing the precious pages. My imagination soars, I can be anyone I want to be, I'm free! My father sees it differently. He figures I'll get dippy from reading the comic books. He tells me to get rid of the junk. I'm shattered. I reluctantly give my life's collection of comics to Davey, a chubby kid up the street. He thanks me like I'm really giving him a great treasure. I don't believe him.

A few days later, I run away from home. No money, no plan. I hitchhike to Bakersfield, sleep in an open field at night. I'm gone for two days. The Highway Patrol picks me up, they notify my father. A few hours later my father comes for me. He looks at me sadly, doesn't say a word. Fact is, I'm a grown man before he mentions what happened with the comic books and me running away and all.

A couple of weeks later I land a job shining shoes at Tillie's Barber Shop in downtown Burbank. We're smack in the middle of a war and seventy-five percent of the customers are servicemen. I feel comfortable in a barbershop amidst the bottles of hair tonic and the keen smell of shaving lotion and face powder. I'm familiar with these things. I figure it's the barbershop where my lifelong curiosity about people was planted.

There is a step-up, two-seater shoeshine stand at the front of the shop. Sam, the Sephardic Jew for whom I work, has been shining shoes for over fifty years and has managed to put two of his sons through college. Sam rarely cracks a smile, he looks sour, but he's really a pussycat. There are two other shops across the street from us. At the entrance of one of the shops, John "The Greek" holds forth with an impressive four-seater shoeshine stand. Adjacent to the stand is a burnished tobacco station. John is quintessentially Greek—happy, sad, bright, crying, laughing, sometimes all at once. Like I said, quintessentially Greek.

A few doors down from the Greek, there's another barbershop, "Vinnie's." There's a three-seater in front of it with two Black guys shining shoes. They really have it together. Incredible, dazzling virtuosos—when they shine shoes it's a performance. Clacking brushes, snapping and popping rags, gently slapping shoe polish onto shoes, all in a toe-tapping rhythm. I'm fascinated with these guys. When I'm not busy, I dash across the street and hang around digging their masterful trip. Sam doesn't approve of the "Shvartza" nonsense. "Too much noise," he growls and tells me to stay put. I cool it when Sam is around—when he's not, I'm popping and snapping my rag like mad.

Tillie, the personable, benign boozer/barber/owner of the shop, is teaching me how to "read people." "Barbers are like monkeys picking bugs off each other. Only we call it grooming. Ya see, grooming is based on love. Monkeys groom each other. That's pretty much what barbers do. Groom people. Ya wanna know people?"

I'm nodding yeah.

"The mirror."

"The mirror?" I naively echo.

"Right. With the mirror, ya learn to see a person's true feelings. Ya can't hide a thing from the mirror. Sees everything. If your eye twitches, the mirror catches it. If your skin changes color, the mirror catches it. Every itsy-bitsy muscle that moves on your face, mirror's right there, on the job. Good, bad, smart, dumb, whatever—mirror don't give a shit. Ey, I can tell from a glance in the mirror if someone is for real, or bullshitting me."

1949

Van Nuys, California. I'm fifteen years old. Three monstrous adolescent years have rolled by. For the last couple of years, my father has been teaching me to play guitar (if I make a mistake he slaps my hand with a wooden spoon), mostly Italian music, but lately I'm into traditional and modern jazz. I'm reading philosophy, science fiction and metaphysical stuff. My eyes are wide open. It's a time when patterns are not yet set and I've not yet been hammered into accepting everything as immutable and hopeless. The world is infinite and mysterious; it's a time of wonder and innocence. I'm a dreamer, I don't fit into dreary schoolrooms. I'm out of sync with the world around me.

Much to my father's dismay, I quit school, forge my birth certificate and, along with my friend and neighbor Stan Bohrman, join the Air Force. Stan is a dead ringer for Tyrone Power (remember him?). He's voted the most popular guy in our school (Van Nuys High), has his own dance band (plays drums), and is bright, wholly charming—and a first-rate snob. (In future years, Stan became a TV reporter and news commentator. He and Regis Philbin had a show together). We swear in and immediately rail to San Antonio, Texas for basic training at Lackland Air Force Base.

The unabashed sun beats on my now shaved head. I'm hot, I'm sweaty, I'm tired. Stan and I are billeted with a bunch of hardcore rednecks. These guys are trucking in another cosmos. I don't see how one could slap or shake them awake. I'm definitely resonating on a different vibration. Maybe I'm haunted.

Since Stan has had ROTC training, he's given a piercing whistle, a shiny-black pith helmet, a pair of snappy white gloves, and is promptly promoted to squad leader. Now snobby Stan shies away from me like a cat from a dog. He lives in the atmosphere of the "privileged, the remarkable."

All the bullshit movies romanticizing the Armed Services are just that, bullshit. I don't even want to think about it. Suffice it to say, the membrane between the world of the Air Forces and my world grew thin and transparent. I could never become a soldier, could never kill anyone. Who could do such a thing? At my age? At any age? A year later, I make damn sure the proper officials find out that I'm underage. I get an Honorable (Minority) Discharge — and I'm gone.

It doesn't take me long to figure out the next move. Barber College. Skid row. The area is full of reeking winos, misfits and lost souls. More basic training, then six months later I'm a barber. My first job. Working for Steve Rangraves in a little two-chair shop in the San Fernando Valley.

Steve is about thirty-five years old, meticulous, well-bred, a good barber too. I'm learning a lot from him. I figured I'd go to Barber College, six months later get my barber's license and I'd be a barber. Bullshit. I learned how to cut hair in Barber College, but cutting hair in the real world is another thing altogether. I don't know shit about cutting hair in a barbershop. Like how to cut hair in a matter of minutes in order to make a living. Or how to not stress out when dealing with the public. Things you don't learn in Barber College.

Three years down the line. I'm nineteen. I get married to Robby King, a nice Jewish girl. Her father is Joe King, a wardrobe man for the motion picture studios. He's won a couple of awards, for "Cyrano de Bergerac" and "High Noon." With me he's kind and avuncular, although he can be bluntly trenchant. On the other hand, his wife is absolutely glacial to me, a four-star bitch. She never accepts the lowly barber marrying her college-educated daughter.

We have a baby girl. The marriage lasts a year and a half. It was doomed from the get-go. We get a divorce—it breaks my heart. I feel like shit. Life is shit. I don't know what the hell life is. I know it can get fucked up—but the sad part? The sorrowful stuff? That's hard to work out...Sempre avanti.

1953

I'm drafted into the Army and sent to Fort Ord in Monterey, California. I become a cook. The good part is, I'm introduced to the magnificent Monterey Peninsula, Carmel and Pacific Grove—but the army is fucking horrendous. A year and a half later, I'm honorably discharged. Another marriage. A son. A divorce. The usual mundane syndrome. I'm working in a little barbershop in the Valley (Van Nuys)— it's a union shop and I'm an upstanding union guy.

I'm given a counting clicker and a picket sign, then promptly dispatched to the entrance of a non-union, cut-rate barbershop (where eight barbers charge a buck a haircut) to click and count the number of people entering the shop. Like I said, I'm a union guy, so I get to work clicking and counting the hairy folks entering the shop. Four hours later and to my astonishment, I've clicked off three hundred and five people. That's more than the shop I'm working in does in an entire week. These guys are snipping in high gear. The haircuts are for shit, but nobody seems to give a damn. It's cheap, that's all that matters. Common sense overwhelms me. If people don't give a shit about getting inferior haircuts, why should I? I dump my picket sign in a nearby trash can, go into the shop and ask for a job.

Supercharged hair clippers whining at high speed sound like the starting line at the Indianapolis 500 auto race. I'm hired and immediately put to work. I thought I was a pretty fast cutter, but these barbers put me to shame—they're doing three haircuts to my one. It takes me six months before I have my speed-cutting chops down. My quickness does not go unnoticed. I'm hired by cut-rate barber chains and sent to various shops to speed up the barbers, like the fastest-gun-in-the-west thing. It wasn't easy, most barbers resented my presence, but I'm learning how to deal with touchy egos to get the job done.

After a couple of years of cut-rate barbering for someone else, I scrape up enough money to open my own mini-chain—five barbershops in Gardena, California, home of the poker casinos—where I charge a dollar and ten cents per haircut.

Three years slip by. I've had it. The hell with barbering. It's a completely different thing nowadays. There's a host of reasons for me quitting the business. For one, women—they've invaded the barbershop. The atmosphere with men among men has vanished. The fine balance between men and women has been abrogated. As Tillie the barber said, "Women are different from men. I'm not against women, they've got a right to be anywhere they want to be, but when it comes to a barbershop, no." I go along with Tillie's salient words, it's a different thing. The particular atmosphere of men with men is gone as soon as you drop a female in there with them. Everything changes. I know, that's a dumb reason for ending my illustrious haircutting career. The real reason is, I'm bored. Ho-hummed out. And since I'm not exactly trying to breast the tape in the business, I'm ready to hang it up.

Enough of this digression. Let's get back to me musing outside Sebring's hair salon, where Rick wants us to get jobs. Busting to go in, Rick springs out of the car and waits for me to do the same. I'm not really into it at all. I'm jaded with the haircutting business. With lingering reluctance, I slowly ease out of the car and join him.

Ten seconds later, I'm facing the front door of the salon on which a big glass-stained ankh fatefully hangs. I'm getting curious now. A hefty push on the door and I'm catapulted into another world. I feel like a country clod come to town. A fetid heat permeates the small cramped room. Music blares with Ray Charles singing "What'd I Say." There's gotta be at least twenty people, all of them keyed to a pitch. The air is laden with vanity and desire, it's a veritable "Who's who" of Hollywood. Henry Fonda; Rich Widmark; Milton Berle, Steve Allen; George Hamilton; Burt Reynolds, like that. I'm dazzled. I don't know what the hell is going on, I mean, what kind of a barbershop is this? Forget the "street barbershop" bullshit. This Sebring guy has something heavy going on, something new and different in the men's haircutting business.

This is nothing like any barbershop I've ever known. Right off, I notice that there's no price list. The nature of commercial barbering is speed. Volume. The more hair you cut the more money you make. Sebring is the opposite of that. While I'm getting a dollar and ten cents a haircut, Sebring is getting seventy-five bucks a haircut, and his staff of a half-a-dozen hairstylists are getting fifteen to twenty-five dollars a haircut. You do the math. The entire concept of men's haircutting is different. When you charge seventy-five bucks a cut you are no longer charging a price, you are charging a fee. They are no longer customers, they are clients. And this shop is totally unique insofar as ninety percent of the clients are into creativity in one form or another. Famous and not so famous actors, producers, directors, writers—artists all. It's not like you're rubbing elbows with a telephone repairman or a corset maker—

not that there's anything wrong with that—it's simply a turn-on to have these creative people hanging around in one small room. It's totally unique and Sebring is the nucleus, he brings the whole thing together. Yeah, this is a place I definitely want to be.

I'm intrigued, I'm interested. I'm grinning from ear to ear. Rick rolls his eyes to Sebring who's cutting Steve McQueen's hair. Sebring is silent, concentrating, absorbed in his work. He's of slender build, dark hair, looks like a bullfighter. I've seen a few great barbers in my day, but this guy leaves them all in the dust. I'm watching his lithe hands dance over Steve McQueen's starry head.

A male receptionist informs Sebring of our arrival. He turns around, spots us, smiles, stops cutting hair and joins us extending his hand. His handshake is untrembling and direct.

"Hi, Jay Sebring." Then he says, "Is this the guy that can do a one-minute haircut?"

"Sure is," declares Rick.

What the hell is he talking about? I'm eyeing Rick for an explanation, instead his face flattens into a distant expression.

With the eagerness of a child, Sebring asks me, "Can you really do it, man?"

"Yeah, but it's nothing like you're doing here. It's a regular garden-variety, street-shop haircut," I manage to mumble. Sebring gives me a sly grin. I'm standing here full of contradictory emotions, my mind buzzing like a bee in a jar of honey.

"Hold on a minute while I finish McQueen," says Sebring. Sebring returns to Steve McQueen, who looks less than patient with the delay in his haircut. I feel like a real jerk. Here I am smack in the middle of "Hollywood," my face a foot away from Paul Newman. Everyone is preening themselves and trying to look casual at the same time. It's all a joke. But I can't summon enough presence to laugh. I lay a heavy look on Rick. He reads my mind.

"You were the entree, man. He wasn't exactly bubbling over with joy to see us until I told him about you. Then I arranged for an audition."

"Audition! You mean, like for a part in a movie? Jesus, man, you don't think, I mean, you don't suppose he'll ask me to cut someone's hair now, do you?"

Rick pops a fresh stick of gum into his mouth and gets into a serious chomp.

"Really man, you don't suppose he will ask me to do that—I mean, right here, the haircut-in-a-minute thing—do you think? These people are megastars, man. I figure I'd kinda like to slide into this Hollywood scene cool, not like some sort of sideshow act."

"You were the entree, man. What can I say?"

Over Rick's shoulder, I can see Sebring has finished cutting Steve McQueen. Now Sebring motions for someone to lower the music, then he steps to the center of the room and raises his arm for attention.

"Folks, listen up." The room becomes still, all eyes on him. "Today we have with us the world's fastest barber. He's going to give us a demo of a one-minute haircut." Murmurs of anticipation from the folks. "We need a model. Who will volunteer?" asks Sebring.

"Volunteer! Christ, he's making it sound like a commando raid or something," I whisper to Rick. There is a cognitive pause. No one is particularly eager to have his hallowed locks defiled by a speeding barber.

"I will," pipes one of Sebring's hairdressers, "Bet you a hundred dollars you can't cut my hair in a minute."

"Bet," cries Rick.

Now folks are exchanging bets. Sebring is grinning gleefully, obviously delighted with the way things are going.

"Please don't fuck up, I have about twenty bucks in my pocket," Rick informs me out of the corner of his mouth.

I read the volunteer as a first-rate, troublemaking asshole with a head of hair like a buffalo. He lays a surly, supercilious look on me. Now I really want to peel this jerk-off.

"What will you need?" asks Sebring.

"A comb and a clipper," I confidently reply.

Sebring snaps his fingers—quick rhythmic snaps. "Kicky, man."

The dramatic tonsorial moment grows nearer. The cutting implements are gingerly laid out on a fresh towel. The uptight model flops onto the cutting chair. I flourish the haircloth, swooping it over his massive head and onto his rigid shoulders. Now the room becomes still, centered, all eyes pinned to my skinny ass. It's a hell of a moment and I wish I were in New Guinea or somewhere. I pick up the comb, flick the switch on the clipper and mercilessly buzz-attack his voluminous head of hair, clumps of which unceremoniously fall to the floor. The guy is transfixed. Zap, zip, now I'm moving to the other side of this head whacking off wads of hair along the way. A few more dazzling moves on top, bing-a-bing, and I'm done. One minute flat.

The guy is livid. "My hair! What the hell did you do?" he squeals like he was just neutered. He tightens his fist threateningly.

Sebring steps between us and tells the punk to chill and pay the money. I tell him to forget about it. I don't want his money. Sebring looks pleased as he takes me aside. "Good street-haircut, man. A tad short for him though. Tell you the truth, man, I didn't think you could do it. But you did. Kicky, man. What sign are you?"

"Leo", I answer, "Leo."

"Cool. Married?"

"Yeah, but it's not happening. I'm getting a divorce."

"Cool. Where do you live?

"The Valley. Van Nuys."

"That's a pity. Move upstairs, man. I got an extra apartment right next door to mine. Be close to the scene."

"Am I in?"

"Sure man. You and your partner. If you want to be."

I'm aching for a change in my life, I eagerly accept his offer. We shake hands, Sebring takes a few steps, then turns to me and grins. "Leo, huh." For a moment he just stares at me, then breaks out in a risible grin.

1961

A year passes. It's been enlightening. I feel like someone has just dumped a pail of ice cold water onto my head. I'm learning a great deal about men's haircutting from Jay (we're on a first name basis now). The man has definitely mastered the art of hair snippery. For months, I sit on a stool and diligently watch him cut. I'm totally absorbed in his method and concept for cutting men's hair.

Jay struts around like he's royalty with his entourage of half-a-dozen people—lawyer, publicist, secretary, a couple of actors—all kissing his ass. If anything is against his wishes, he becomes morose, his hands clasped behind his back, a la Groucho Marx. In spite of his outrageous moods, he's a true-blue, good soul. Jay and his stunningly beautiful wife Camy, who's in her early twenties, are in the next apartment, a few feet away from my door. Camy spends at least nineteen hours a day in the bathroom, patting, powdering and painting her face and lithe body.

Meanwhile, in my own life, through a musician friend, I meet the person who changes my life forever. Marilyn Brown. Twenty years old, big tits and bright blue eyes. She's a makeup artist, high-line stuff, Beverly Hills. At the risk of sounding corny, I sensed a real Kismet thing happening the moment I was alone with her. In no time, we're getting-it-on, eye-to-eye and heart-to-heart. That's another thing I quickly discovered, that her heart is as big as her bosom, and her mind as bright as her eyes.

Since Jay lives just a few feet away, he invariably pops in on Marilyn and me—usually around one or two in the morning—practically demanding a cup of coffee and a nosh. After which, he goes into a rant full throttle, quick, graphic and peppered with humor. He rants and raves, but underneath the raving is heavy satire which adds a heady ambiguity to his words. His rants are never boring, however, after an hour or two, the words pile up and it wipes me out. When he finely leaves, Marilyn and I collapse onto my crummy rented couch/bed utterly spent.

For the first few months that's the way it goes. I didn't reveal my true self to Jay, fearing I would blow the gig if I laid out my honest feelings about stuff straight and undiluted. So, wanting to keep the gig and continue the Hollywood-thing going, I remain tacitly cool.

But my coolness was nowhere to be found at two o'clock one particular morning when Jay's demanding knock on the door ruffled my Sicilian fur. I had a really bad day and was in no mood for Jay's usual acrimonious rants. I lay it out straight—telling him to go fuck himself and get the hell out of my apartment. Jay leaves without saying a word. That's it. I've just blown the gig. For sure that's what I've just done. Blown it. Dejected, I pull the sheets over my dumb hot head.

It doesn't turn out that way at all. The following morning, Jay is as sweet as Grandma's cannoli. From this day forward I don't hold back a single syllable from him. He asks me a straight question, I give him a straight answer. Life is easier that way.

Jay asks me if I would like to accompany him on a house call that evening. Hell yes, that's an honor, going to a star's domain, watching the master working his silky smooth haircutting expertise. I want to get there myself someday. Right now, I'm content witnessing the Hollywood dream surreally floating by. How should I dress? Jay tells me to wear the same thing I have on. It's the uniform we all wear in the barbershop, denim shirt and pants, not unlike county jail attire.

It's nighttime, I'm tapping on Jay's door. Camy answers. She's quiet, fragile, a couple of quick hellos, and I'm in. I settle down and wait for Jay. I'm the world's worst waiter, can't wait for shit. Here I am waiting for him like a trained seal.

"Be there in a flash, man," sings Jay from the bathroom. Jay senses my impatience. "There's a number in the ashtray."

I spot the number, light up, have a hit. Camy drifts by, has a couple of dreamy puffs, says something to me and drifts away. I don't know what the hell she said—she has this tiny voice like an insect—I'm straining to catch a few words here and there. Enter the dapper Jay Sebring, a wide grin for me, and then he turns to Camy.

"Watch?"

I see Camy's lips move, but I don't know what the hell she's saying. I guess Jay does—he returns to the bathroom and fetches his wristwatch.

"Ring?"

Again her lips move, but not a word do I catch. Now Jay goes into the bedroom and fetches his ring. I kick back. The way things are going, it's going to be awhile before we actually get out the door and on our way.

Half an hour later, we're in Jay's brand new Lincoln Continental, listening to a blaring Frank Sinatra tape. He's singing, "Fly Me To The Moon." Zoom, zam, we're on our way. Jay is driving like a amphetamined astronaut, weaving in and out of traffic practically running cars off the freeway. I feign composure and wait until it's reasonably safe to speak, lest I distract him from his madman maneuvering. After awhile, when things are conducive to conversation, I ask, "Where we going, man?"

"Palm Springs."

"Whose house?"

"Ol' Blue Eyes."

"Who's Blue Eyes?"

"Sinatra, man."

"Frank?"

"Ol' fuckin' Blue Eyes," says Jay as he inserts another Sinatra tape into the player. He chuckles to himself, then drifts away into his own thoughts. I do the same. For awhile, we drive along, save the Sinatra tape, in complete silence. We split a number.

"How about one side of the head cut like Auschwitz, the other side cut real neat, like a businessman's thing, only have a long oiled sideburn, with a little cricket cage hanging on the end of the sideburn, with a wacko cricket singing 'Old Man River,'" says Jay.

"Or 'o Solo Mio,'" I mumble.

Jay breaks into a full smirk, then bam! My seat abruptly drops back into a launching position. I'm startled. He cracks up laughing. "I guess I pressed the wrong gizmo." A few feral turns and we're on the back roads of Palm Springs. "You into whipping chicks, man?" asks Jay.

"No, not really. You never know though. I might change my mind next week. But I tell ya, man, I can't take the lash. I'm a giver," I reply.

Jay almost clips an errant rabbit hopping across the road. "I'm going to have a torture chamber in my next pad, man. All the kicky stuff. Chains, screws, ropes, hoods, whips. Eh, man?"

I let it hang.

Now he starts tapping his fingers on the dashboard. "Wanna meet an artist?" asks Jay.

"A painter artist?"

"Right. A painter."

"How about Ol' Blue Eyes?"

Jay's eyes pop wide open. "Fuck, man. Shit! Fuck. I completely forgot about ol' Blue Eyes." He stomps on the gas pedal.

We arrive an hour late for ol' Blue Eyes. At the front gate, a salty black guy tells Jay to forget about it. Ol' Blue Eyes is seriously pissed. We split.

Jay is fuming. "Who the hell is he anyhow?" bleats Jay. He slams the pedal to the floorboard, honking at slower moving vehicles. "Who the hell does he think he is?"

Now we're up to a hundred and ten miles an hour and climbing. Jay senses my tension, smirks sadistically. I shut my eyes, resigned to the finger of fucking fate.

"Fuck his ass," he says as he inserts a Tony Bennett tape. "Fuck him." Now he sparks a doobie, has a couple of hits and passes it to me. "Fuck him," he says with a deflating sigh followed by a pensive pause.

"Wanna fall by this artist's place, man?" he asks.

"Sure, why not?" I say.

"You'll dig him. He's out there, man. Way out. Out to-ronney."

A half-hour later, the Continental is sliding in on a cloud of night desert dust—a swerve, a roll, a dip, finally coming to a jarring halt in front of a ramshackle cabin. The silence is palpable.

"We're in the smackness of nowhere," I whisper to Jay. Jay just sits there, unmoved, like a hunk of alabaster. Suddenly a loud throaty roar jiggles the car's dashboard.

"What the hell is that?" I fearfully ask.

"A lion," Jay replies calmly.

"A wha'?"

"A lion. I told you the dude is out there, man."

"The guy has a lion? A real lion?"

Jay looks at me and grins sardonically.

A couple of hours later the four of us—me, Jay, a funky effete artist and a squatting lion—are sitting on the dirt floor of the cabin, munching on a pile of peyote buttons. The lion yawns, then stares hard at me like I'm prey. Momento mori...

❦

I'm cutting Sam Cooke, one of my favorite clients. Sam is ultra-cool—quiet, unpretentious, a delightful and generous guy. Jay sticks his head out of his private cutting room, catches my exhausted red eyes, winks elfishly, makes circles around his ears and pantomimes the words "mass hypnosis," then retreats into his room. I'm trying to concentrate on cutting Sam's hair—I'm straining. Sam senses my woeful condition.

"You're a little shaky, Sal. Want to do the cut tomorrow?" Sam softly asks.

"I'll be cool when the music stops. It's got me dippy, man."

The Bolero mercifully ends, for which I'm infinitely grateful. Gypsy Boots spots Sam, comes over and says hello. Gypsy is kind of a celebrity around town. He's a hardcore vegetarian/naturalist who's frequently on the Steve Allen show pushing the "natural" lifestyle. He's sandaled, tanned, long-haired and gabby. Sam, always affable, buys a couple of veggie sandwiches from him. Gypsy splits.

For a moment the shop is still. Then a piercing scream rattles my brain. Then "Power! Power!" What the hell is it?

I spin around to see a slovenly guy in his early fifties—greasy, rumpled suit, oily hair, needing a shave, four inches of ash hanging from his smoldering cigarette. And in tandem with him, a half-a-dozen people—a mixture of beautiful broads, aspiring actors, and high-line hairdressers. This guy is shouting to everyone in the shop. "Power! Power! What do we do with it?" he carries on. Everyone in the shop is pinned to him. Now he lowers his voice and confidentially whispers, "You're all dreaming. Dreaming. Sleepers sleeping, sleeping. Awake! awake!"

Folks are hammered by his every word. He comes closer to me, squints hard, assays my total being.

"You Leo. Wake Up. Lions sleep too much," he says in a sotto voce rasp.

Before I can respond, he bounds into Jay's room. Sam turns to me and asks, "So what's your sign?"

"Leo. How'd he know, man?"

"He's something else. A master."

"He looks like a vagrant."

"He has a shampoo company called Lapinal."

"What's his name?"

"Al Lapin."

Over Sam's shoulder, I see Al Lapin bolting out of Jay's room, practically dragging the docile Cliff Robertson through the shop and outside to the bright sunshine for a closer look at his hair (Jay has just finished dying Cliff's hair for the role of John F. Kennedy in the movie "PT-109"). He motions for me to join him. A few more snips on Sam's hair and I'm done. "I gotta check this guy out, man," I confide to Sam.

"Watch yourself, man. The man can mess with your head."

I say goodbye to Sam and join Mr. Lapin outside the shop.

"Come here, Leo!" commands Al as he sticks his nose in my face. "Wake up! Lions sleep too much," he says to me in a confidential grunt. Then bam! He pops into a sweaty rant. "Hair! Think hair! Think. Quick. Fuck 'em all. All of them!" Now he lowers his head onto his chest and giggles. He's satisfied with himself, as if he thought of a punch line to a joke not yet conceived.

Twenty minutes later, Jay, Al and I are huddling over my rented coffee table. Al, sans his flowery entourage, is demonstrating his technique of rolling a joint with one hand, while spewing on and on about Dianetics (precursor to Scientology)—the clears, engrams, whatever. We rap for a couple of hours. He comes on like a battalion of steamrollers.

CHAPTER TWO

My childhood fantasies of meeting and talking to movie stars has become an everyday reality. To name a few coming into the shop: Peter Lawford, wired; Chuck Connors, crotch checker; James Garner, affable, regular guy; Rod Sterling, pensive; Swifty Lazar, pompous; Burt Reynolds, amped; George Hamilton, in the shop a couple times a week, neat guy, keen sense of humor; Bob Goulet, unassuming; Richard Widmark, quiet, guarded; Gregory Peck, regal, a powerful presence; Jackie Cooper, modest; Tony Bennett, ya' gotta like this, man, he's generous and down to earth; Richard Burton, suave, looks right through you with his boozy eyes; Steve Allen, vigilantly vain; Prince Rainier, effortless charm; Robert Conrad, humble, treats you like a human being, tells you about his days as a milkman; Richard Chamberlain, crotch checker; Jules Stein, pale, sullen.

With Milton Berle, the world is his audience. He's always acting, never without an overcoat—it could be ninety degrees, he's wearing his battered overcoat—doing shtick, looking for the laugh. Behind Jackie Mason's smile I sense an impregnable petulance. Henry Mancini has an innate elegance.

Sammy Davis never comes on like a star, is easy to be with and has a diabolic sense of humor. I did a few house calls at his modest house above Sunset Blvd. It's usually a morning call and his wife, Mae Britt, always has a warm pleasant smile as she greets me at the front door and steers me into a cramped den. In a matter of minutes, Sammy slips into the room half-stoned with a malt-size glass of booze. While I'm cutting his hair he runs old movies, Charlie Chan and Buck Rogers.

Marlon Brando has a looming presence. He looks at you as if he's about to bite off your nose, but come to find out, he's hearty and mellow. After a couple of minutes, I feel like I'm talking to my Uncle Louie. He's family.

Henry Fonda, one of my idols, is impeccably well mannered, a gentleman, who prefers to be in the background. He looks you straight in the eye when he talks to you.

Paul Newman is modest, observing, reticent—he and Jay share an interest in racecar driving. Steve McQueen is a stoner, a star, and he knows it. He and Jay are buddies and have an inordinate interest in motorcycle riding.

Bobby Darin is my man. I go to his house in Toluca Lake to do his hair. This is another guy I can completely relax with (he's Italian). He whips off his toupee, I do his hair, we split a doobie. He tells me tales about W.C. Fields who lived across the lake. Each evening W.C. would row around the lake waving to his neighbors, and occasionally he would fall into the lake and swim to shore, still waving to his neighbors.

Artists, writers, psychologists, astrologers, numerologists, spiritualists, producers, directors—it's all happening in the shop, and I'm smack in the middle of it. Jay's vision is unclouded, he wants fame and fortune and he's getting it. His image is plastered in most of the popular magazines, his name is rapidly becoming synonymous with men's hairstyling. About my own trip, I'm in another world now—a completely different lifestyle. Marilyn and I are living together in West Hollywood. She's getting into my head. I love it.

Last night around midnight, I'm kicked back half watching the Steve Allen show, when I hear a familiar "ratta tatta" tapping on my door. Reluctantly, unwinding myself from the sofa, I slowly open the door—it's Jay.

"Just got back from Gotham, man, got any coffee?"

"Tea," is my pithy reply.

"Tea. No coffee?"

"Just tea."

"Where's Marilyn?"

"Late movie with her girlfriend."

"Girlfriend? Man, ya' never know 'bout that. Chicks will tell you all kinds of bullshit. Could be a secret boyfriend. Then you'd get pissed off, get depressed, go to pieces. Then you become depressed, then you walk around getting silly and fucked up. Who knows what the hell you're liable to do?"

"Will you stop that shit," I say. We hug each other.

"Tea...yeah, tea," says Jay.

"So, what's going on, man?" I ask while preparing the tea.

"Fucking New York City, man. It's a groove. Fast, anything you want, chop chop, it's there."

"You cut hair?"

"I did a TV show."

"A demo on TV?"

"No man, I was a guest on a show. A fucking guest."

"Which show?"

"'What's My Line?' fucking 'What's My Line?,' man."

"That's the show where the panel has to figure out who the real you is, right?"

"Right, three of us stand there, they ask us some dumb questions, trying to figure out who the real Jay Sebring is."

"That's a big show, lots of folks tune in on that one, man."

"Millions, catching my profile on the tube. Kicky."

"So, did the panel get it right?"

"Hell no. They picked this girly looking guy. Then they announce that I'm the real Jay Sebring from Hollywood and I do the stars' hair, ta da ta da. Then they ask me a few more questions about hair stuff. A guy on the panel asks me what I would do with his hair? I tell him that I have no idea, that he is too far away and that I would have to take a closer look at his hair."

"Figures," I mutter.

"You would think so. This cat is about fifty fucking feet away from me and he asks what I would do with his hair."

"You're supposed to have eyes like a hawk," I slip in.

"Right. A fucking hawk."

"Flying around the sky, doing nothing."

"Once in awhile, I check out the scene below."

I pour myself and Jay a cup of tea. Jay has a taste, makes a wry face. "I'm moving on, man. Moving on. Shampoo company, men's cosmetics and, get this, a charm school for men."

"Whoa."

"Yeah. Dig it. We teach the guys about total appearance. Their hair, what to wear, how to talk, which fucking fork to use, poetry, karate, foreign language, stock market savvy, how to get laid, cool stuff. New York, Paris, Rome, and you're gonna be right there with me."

I give Jay my wary Sicilian eye that says, "I'll believe it when I see it."

∿

I've just finished a long day on the MGM studio's "Star Trek" set where I've been doing Jeff Hunter's hair. He's a neat guy and a fine actor. He's played leads in many Hollywood films, his most famous role that of Jesus Christ in "King Of Kings." Now he's playing Captain Kirk, the "first" Captain Kirk. Today Jeff told me a story about the time he was playing Jesus Christ in "King Of Kings." A heavy New York City critic hated the movie, hated Jeff's portrayal of Jesus and blasted Jeff with scathing negatives. Jeff responded by writing a letter to the venomous critic saying something like, "You dirty, motherfucking asshole, sonofabitch, fucking pussy-ass cocksucker, dip shit putz," then signed the letter, "Sincerely, Jesus H. Christ."

I bump into Jay on the narrow stairway leading to our respective upstairs apartments. He's juggling a lamp, a world atlas, two hairdryers, and a 30x30 color portrait of himself seriously gazing at the world atlas contemplating our blue planet. "I'm setting up earth-props, man. Got a house in Benedict Canyon, moving out of here," Jay calls to me over his shoulder as he gingerly descends the stairway. "The address is on your kitchen table. Come on by tonight, it's going to freak you, man."

It's night, I'm winding through the illustrious Benedict Canyon. A sharp turn here, a sharp turn there and I'm on a narrow uphill road. Couple more turns and I'm on a long private driveway, at the end of which, nestled in a cozy corner of the hillside, sits a gingerbread house encircled with shady trees and flowery patches that tightly lace the hillside and an oval-shaped swimming pool. Jay is pumped and proud of his house. It's a delight with dark woods, cozy corners, shiny mahogany bannisters.

"Dig this," says Jay as he faces a huge knotty pine bookcase. "This used to be W.C. Fields' pad, man." Now Jay reaches behind the bookcase, presses a hidden button, and presto! The bookcase slowly inverts into a private bar completely stocked, including half-a-dozen stools and tables. "It's soundproofed. W.C. had this secret room built so he could get away from people and still feel like he was in a tavern. Kicky, eh?" We fearlessly step into the secret tavern.

"Wanna drink, man?" Before I can answer, Jay is into it.

"Margarita?" he asks. I nod yes.

"This place cost a few dineros, man. How'd you swing it? Shit, forget what I just asked, man. You swung it. That's cool. Damn cool. I'm probably fuckin' jealous."

"Jinxed, man," says Jay in a flat voice.

"Jinxed? You said jinxed?"

Jay buzzes the noisy-ass, ice-mixing thing—its intrusive clacking dominates the room. I'm waiting for it to stop spinning before I can go on with my life. Now Jay expertly fills my chilled and salted glass, does the same for himself. We raise our glasses high.

"Salute, Salvatore," says Jay.

"Salute, Tom." (Tom is his real name). We silently sip our margaritas.

"Jinxed?" I repeat.

"Yeah. Jinxed. I think it's haunted too," he says refilling our glasses.

"Lay it out, man."

"Back in the early thirties, when Hollywood was party time, some guy named Paul Bern got all spun out on some chick. When Hollywood was hot and people were getting into all kinds of shit."

Jay's laser-keen eyes spot a couple of drops of tequila on the polished wood bar. He wipes it clean with a bar cloth.

"So. What happened?" I pointedly ask.

"So the guy blew his brains out in this house."

"Over a chick?"

"That's what went down, man."

"Who's the chick?"

Jay's face reddens. For a couple of seconds he examines his fingernails. Then he shouts, "Jean Harlow. Jean fuckin' Harlow!" His chest rumbles. "Harlow. Fuckin' Harlow, man." He starts laughing. Hard tears rolling down his cheeks.

I mumble something senseless of no import and laughingly join Jay in, I sense, a prescient irony. Our cryptic mirth slowly subsides. Jay hands me a Kleenex, I wipe my teary eyes, he does the same. There's a pause. Something has just turned over in his mind. I sip my drink and wait for him to speak.

Now he's looking me straight in the eye and in a dour tone says, "Jinxed. Man, everyone that ever lived here has died a tragic death." He turns around and faces a mirror behind the bar, checking out his image as if he's making a promise to himself. For a moment there's a permeating stillness, then he spins around like a cornered mongoose, grins and asks, "More booze, man?"

❧

Months later, I take my first LSD trip at Jay's haunted house (it was still legal). I arrive around eleven o'clock at night. A few people are there—Al Lapin, the artist guy from the desert, a couple of beautiful chicks, Jay and myself. I immediately ask Jay about the LSD. He points to the kitchen table on top of which is a half-gallon jug half full of what looks like gin or vodka.

"That it?" I ask.

"That's it, man."

Jay is preoccupied and heads upstairs to his bedroom and his guests. I sit down at the kitchen table to check out the jug of LSD. I find a shot glass and pour myself a shot of the acid. I look at it. I'm hesitating...I mean this is powerful stuff. Nothing to fuck around with. I'm just about to knock back the shot when I hear Jay's urgent yell behind me.

"No! Stop! Stop! Don't drink it!"

I freeze.

"Man, I forgot to tell you. This is the pure stuff. LSD 25. Two drops is 500 milligrams. That will get you spinning for twelve hours. Just put two drops in some orange juice or something. Sorry, man. I should have told you about that stuff. I'm half here. Ya know?"

I nod as if I know what the hell he's talking about. He splits back upstairs. I find some orange juice, gingerly drip two drops of the acid into the juice. Five minutes later—Bingo! It's like a mental concussion. I freefall into the Zen zone. All is one. We are all one. The mind that does not understand, that mind is the Buddha. Stuff like that. Twenty-four hours later. I'm seriously thrashed. I feel like I've just flown in from another country. I call it a day, find my way home and plop onto my unmade bed.

A few weeks later I'm in the shop cutting hair when I get a phone call. Jay wants to see me. I finish the cut, go upstairs to his apartment. Jay is staring out the window, his hands held contemplatively behind his back. He slowly pivots around and faces me, giving me an amusing look. "The King wants you to cut his hair," croons Jay.

"The King? Who the hell is the King?"

Now Jay chuckles—throws a couple of playful punches to my stomach. "The King!"

"King who?" I repeat.

"The fucking King, man!"

A luminous thought goes through my head. "Frank Sinatra?" I blurt.

"No, man. The fucking King," intones Jay, throwing a few more playful punches to my midsection.

I surrender. "Who?"

"Elvis fucking Presley, man! The fucking Kingo!"

I'm dumbfounded. I'm imagining myself getting down with the King. Jay interrupts my brief reverie.

"Are you ready for the King?"

"How did this come down, man?"

"Sonny West."

"Sonny West. I do his hair. He's cool. Big guy. Soft spoken. A gentleman. I like him."

"Sonny is a member of the Memphis Mafia."

"The what?"

"Memphis Mafia. It's what the press calls the guys working for Elvis. They go everywhere with Elvis. Sonny is one of his three bodyguards. He's known Elvis since their high school days, before the King became famous."

"The King needs three bodyguards?"

"Hey man, freakies out there, jealous freakies. Pissed, because their girlfriends have a snapshot of Elvis in their wallet. Jealous, because the King has it down. Anyhow, Sonny said he's invited you, via the King, several times to come up to his house and play softball with the them. You told Sonny no."

"What the hell do I want with softball?"

"Man, you're being handed a hell of an opportunity. Do you realize that some people would kill to go where you are going?"

"Where am I going?"

"Right beside the King. Sideburn to sideburn! So here's the trip, man. Yesterday you got a call to come up to the King's pad to do his hair. So, the shot is, it wouldn't look too cool for me not to show up on the scene. At least for the first time. The Hollywood press would love to get a hold of something like that. 'Sebring Snubbed For Sub by the King'—that's how the Hollywood press would put it."

"I dig, it's like a King to King thing," I say.

"Here's the deep part, man," Jay says as he grins diabolically. "His hair is fucked. Messed up, man. Looks like someone has been cutting it with a broken bottle. I had to whack it down to the basics. You'll see."

"I'll see? What am I going to see?"

Jay feigns a reassuring smile. "He went white, man. I thought he was going to faint! Man, the cat went fucking white. Snow fucking white." Jay throws a couple of karate punches at an imaginary partner. Then he starts cracking up. It's infectious, I can't hold back. I join him in the releasing laughter.

Next day. I'm driving through the hallowed gates of Bel Air, checking addresses, looking for the King's castle. Everything is big and grand and pleasant—houses, garages, shiny brass doorknobs. I feel separate, like I'm in the army and these people outrank me. The watcher and the watched. Ah money. My Healy rolls smoothly around a flower-laden corner.

I spot a bevy of females ranging in age from fifteen to twenty-five huddled in front of a high-walled mansion and an entrance from which a massive iron gate hangs delineating the great from the ordinary. I recheck the address, yep, this is the place. The King's pad. I have arrived. Zip! In half a second, the flock of females surrounds my car.

"How do you get into this place?" I pointedly ask.

"Press the button on the gate and tell them you're here," squeaks a wide-eyed believer.

"Who are you?" squeals another.

"I'm here to do Elvis' hair."

"Elvis' hairstylist!" yelps another fan.

"Elvis' hairstylist!" the girls scream in concert.

"Can I have a lock of his hair? Please please!" screams another, cleaving my eardrums.

"Me too," begs one of the pinker pinkies.

Another crazed creature seductively spreads herself across the hood of my car. Now I know I'm dealing with a bunch of nuts. "Look, I just do hair, not brain surgery," I say, as I'm urgently pressing the speaker button on the gate. A voice quickly responds. I recognize the voice of Sonny West. "It's me, man. The hair thing. Four o'clock. I'm here."

The gate slowly opens like a monstrous man-eating plant. The giggling girls become still, focused, their eager faces straining for a glimpse on the other side of the gate—The Holy Land.

"Ladies, if you will kindly get out of the way." I push the pedal hard to the floorboard, practically flinging bodies off the car. I zoom through the open gate—a swerve, a screech, and a jarring halt a few feet away from a startled Asian gardener bending over trimming a bed of roses. I get out of the car and courteously bow to him. He bows back.

"Sho, damn, man, y'all in a hurry to see me," drawls Sonny.

"Jesus, what the hell is that all about?" I'm pointing to the pack of feral females at the gated entrance.

"Sorry about that, Saul. Elvis' fans. They're heah all the time, y'all get used to it. Y'all got your haircutting stuff?"

I shake my brown paper bag as I get out of the car.

"Damn, man, y'all need a new bag or something. Come on in see the place. The Shah of Iran used to live heah."

"Really," I reply, acutely underwhelmed.

Is he going to be difficult to deal with? I mean, his hair is his trip, what with the sideburn thing and all. Let's face it. The guy will be impossible to please. I'm getting nervous thinking about it. What the hell am I doing here? I'm getting feverish. I face the gardener and lay another bow on the dude. He bows back.

Following Sonny into the King's castle, I'm escorted to a large circular room surrounded by plump sofas. In the center of the room sits a bright green pool table dominating the room like a huge water lily. Beyond the water lily is a dining room where six guys ranging from twenty to thirty years old are sitting around a king-sized oak table. Laughing, giggling, horsing around. They spot me. All eyes cover me like a butterfly net. There's a long studied pause.

"This heah is Saul, the guy that's been cutting my hair," says Sonny.

"Sal," I correct Sonny.

"Shoo, man, I'm sorry. I always say that, don't I?"

One of the guys, dressed like Zorro, pops up and pumps my hand vigorously, says his name is Gene Smith (he's one of Elvis' many country cousins). He snickers and points to another member of the entourage.

"That thar guy with the big ol' belly is Alan Fortis." Alan slips me a sly smile.

"Over thar is li'l ol' Billy Smith." I get a shy but critical eye contact from a genuine country boy.

"That guy thar is 'The Broom,'" continues Zorro pointing to a rail of a guy who eases out of his chair, smiles brightly and shakes my hand.

"Howdy. Richard Davis is my name. Don't listen to a thang they tell y'all 'bout me. All damn fools, 'cept me," drawls The Broom.

"Looky heah, I'm all doing the meetin' stuff," says Zorro, a tad miffy. "That thar guy next to the Broom is Moon. Damn if that don't rhyme."

"Marty Laker, it's my bald head. So the Moon," responds an intense, balding, banjo-eyed member of the gang.

"The other skinny guy thar," Zorro points, "is Jim Kingsley."

Jim smiles politely, steeples his finger and nods.

"Where's Joe? Does he know Saul is heah?" asks Sonny.

A wave of panic flows through the room. The guys look at each other for an answer. "Phone him up," pipes Li'l Billy.

Alan darts to a phone and is about to dial, when a cool voice over my shoulder asks, "Elvis up yet?" The guys sigh with relief. It's easy to figure the voice I hear is the alpha male of this pack. I turn and see a guy in his late twenties, casually dressed, with dark hair and dark clear eyes. "I'm Joe Esposito," he says introducing himself.

"Sal Orefice."

"Italian?"

"What else. You?"

"Me too."

"Where?"

"New York till eleven, then Los Angeles. You?"

"Chicago. Everything all right?"

"Everything is fine."

Joe faces the guys squarely. "Anyone check on Elvis?"

The guys launch into an explosive volley of words, each claiming the other goofed at his job. In the midst of the confusion, as if a secret trapdoor has been opened, Elvis magically appears, with a little guy standing beside him. Airy hypocrisy and forced sincerity bounce off the walls. Everyone except Joe snaps to attention. Elvis is dressed in a black one-piece jumpsuit, replete with dangling bracelets, leather wristbands, diamond-ringed fingers, black shiny boots, dark sunglasses and a beat-up skipper's cap. Looking into his eyes, I catch a glimpse of a war going on in his mind and his smile. I don't know if he's laughing or crying.

"Sal, I'd like you to meet Elvis Presley," says Joe.

"Hi, man," says the King, warmer than I thought he would be. We shake hands. It's a firm handshake without pomp.

"This is Charlie Hodge," Elvis indicates the little guy standing beside him.

"Hi," I laconically reply.

Elvis sighs, the guys tighten. Now he reaches into his pocket, comes up with a long twisty cigar—the guys move as if on radar, scrambling to light the stogie. Charlie Hodge is the lucky one.

"Glad you could make it, man. It's my hair," he stammers self-consciously, "Can you take a look at it?"

"My pleasure, Mr. Presley."

"Elvis, man. Elvis," says the King, putting me at ease.

"Where would you like me to do it?" I ask.

Elvis' face heightens, not knowing how to answer such a mundane question. The guys stir, anticipating the next desire/wish to be instantly fulfilled.

"What do you need, man?" Elvis asks me.

"Light would be nice."

"How about the bathroom?" Joe softy suggests.

"Is that alright?" Elvis anxiously asks me.

"Sounds good to me."

Now I'm following Elvis, Charlie and Joe down a long dark hallway which leads to a huge bathroom with a closet half the size of a bowling alley in which a dazzling array of clothing mutely hangs. Charlie graciously directs me to a suitable spot in front of a large three-way mirror. In front of the mirror, he strategically places a chair and a small table onto which he sets an electric shaver, a book (I can't see the title), and a bottle of Pepsi, which Elvis contemplatively pours into an iced glass.

"How's that?" Charlie asks me.

"Perfect. Thank you," I say, hoping my reply is well disposed.

Charlie crosses to the bathroom clothes hamper, onto which he perches like a molting blue jay. I learn that Charlie is from Alabama, a backup singer and guitarist with several prominent country groups. He's also Elvis' court jester.

I lay out my haircutting paraphernalia and wait for the King to sit. For a couple of minutes, Elvis circles the chair like a suspicious animal. Finally, he pounces onto the chair with a resigned sigh. He yanks the skipper's cap off his head and flings it across the bathroom. Charlie immediately retrieves the hat and sets it onto the clothes hamper. Elvis avoids looking directly at the mirror. I don't blame him, his hair looks like a damp clump of black spinach. It's a mess. I don't know if I can resurrect his locks. I may be in deep trouble. Whatever haircutting skills I've developed in my stellar career are hereby immediately summoned.

Suddenly, Elvis bolts out of the chair and nervously paces in front of the mirror while shaking his hands vigorously at his sides. His brow furrows, he's frustrated and undecided. It's gotta be a big thing, in his life—his hair. The sideburn thing, for sure. I wait patiently while the King goes through what-the-hell-ever Kings go through. He reexamines the chair as if it were a booby trap.

"If this were an electric chair, man, I'd be gone. Amp my ass clean across the border. Gone, man. Gone!"

Charlie, right on cue, jumps in on the tirade. "Damn right, E. Damn right," Charlie laughs.

"I'd end up in some ol' taco or burrito or some shit, man."

"Some ol' senora make a tamale stew out of y'all," quips Charlie.

"Tamale stew? Man, you better quit sniffing that hairspray or some other shit y'all sniffing. Tamale stew?"

"Burned," says Charlie. (When anyone says or does something stupid, the guys say "burned.")

I listen, I wait. After a few minutes of some snappy banter, I'm chortling right along with them. Some funny stuff goes down. Finally, Elvis reluctantly reseats himself, picks up the electric razor and begins gliding the razor over his famous face.

I get down to business, wash his hair, a snip here and there, a blow dryer thing, etc. All the time, Elvis is either shaving, sipping on a glass of ice water or reading his book on astrology. Relaxed. Vulnerable. Never once did he look into the mirror. He sits quietly until the very end of my tonsorial endeavor before he raises his head and looks into the mirror. For few seconds he studies his reflection and then I hear, "Thank you very much." That said, the King happily (I hope) departs with Charlie hot on his heels.

Now I'm alone stuffing my haircutting gear into my brown paper bag. Have I reached the apex of my career in the King's toilet? A doorknob rattles. In walks Joe. "How'd it go?" he asks.

"It worked out."

"Elvis liked what you did with his hair. He wants to know if you can come to the studio tomorrow morning and do his hair?"

I sense an opportunistic door being opened into a world of super people with super bathrooms, super cars, super clothes, super dilemmas. This is my chance to check out the "sho-biz" thing. "Can do," I cheerfully reply.

When I return to my apartment, Marilyn asks me what Elvis is like. "Complex" is the first thing that comes to my mind.

The movie Elvis is shooting is called "Fun In Acapulco." It's my first day on the set at Paramount Studios. I'm tripping. The dank smell of the huge stages. Wires, cables, dollies, cameras, lights and, of course, the actors and directors—the ones that save us from the boredom and inanities of everyday living. Movies give us glory, hope and pleasure—as seen through the eyes of the dreamers, the creators.

When I was a kid in the Bronx, about ten or eleven, it was movies, at least twice a week, sometimes three, where I was planted at one of the local theaters. A double feature, a weekly serial ("The Green Hornet"), a newsreel and a cartoon. That added up to a lot of viewing.

As soon as I step into the studio stage, my mind spins into reverse and I'm in that Bronx movie theater, whiffing the same musty air and seeing myself sitting in the last row in a corner seat, my hands on my cheeks, my eyes pinned to the screen, anticipating another great movie. But, I gotta tell you, once you see how moviemaking is actually done, it kind of ruptures your imagination. Still, flicks are great, and I'm compelled to observe the moviemaking process as it's happening.

At the moment, I'm planted watching Elvis doing a matte shot (i.e., a camera shot that produces a contrived effect, combining a pre-photographed background with a live action scene). Elvis is wearing swimming trunks and he's about to do a swan dive off a treacherous one-hundred-foot cliff into the churning ocean below. Standing precariously on the cliff edge, Elvis shakes his pale arms at his sides, takes a deep breath, raises his arms above his head, bends over swooping his arms forward, and bravely dives off the cliff into the awaiting ocean. Actually, he stepped forward about a foot off camera—Cut! They fill in later with a professional double doing the real diving.

Immediately after shooting the scene, Elvis—followed by Joe Esposito and Charlie Hodge—skitters to his dressing room. A half a minute later, I'm summoned. What's with the King? His hair looked good in the scene. What? Grabbing my paper bag of hair gear, I'm on my way. Entering the dressing room, I see Elvis sitting at the makeup table facing the mirror, looking absolutely somber.

"I just dived off a cliff into a cold-ass ocean," says Elvis.

"Right," I knowingly respond.

"My hair has to be wet for the next scene."

Moments like this I don't know what the hell I'm supposed to do. Elvis hates to get his hair wet. I know it. He knows it. Few people have seen Elvis' hair wet. It's like a phobia thing with him.

"Wet?" I ask softly.

"But not too wet," says Elvis patting the back of his head.

"Like semi-wet?" I ask.

"Like some ol' semi-truck," Elvis mumbles.

"Some ol' car wash, fer y'all's hair," quips Charlie.

"Pull up in a long-ass limo, stick my head out the window and get a shampoo," continues Elvis.

"Hot wax too," quickly injects Charlie.

"Ten minutes," says Joe to Elvis.

"Okay, Sal. Do something with my hair," says Elvis.

"Why don't I spritz a little bit at a time, you tell me when to stop." Elvis looks puzzled. "Spritz. It's a Jewish thing."

Elvis nods his head knowingly. I get right to it. I spritz, I comb, I spritz, I comb—then pause for his comment, which I hope is forthcoming.

He looks hard at his image. "Li'l more," he mumbles.

Back to it. Spritz, comb, pause, wait.

Elvis checks out his hair, then nods his approval. "Good," says Elvis, then to Joe and Charlie, "Let's hit it."

They leave. I pack up my hair stuff and retreat into the shadows to view the shooting of the following scene in which Elvis, after his impressive dive, emerges triumphantly from the ocean—actually a small, ad hoc swimming pool—his quaff, meticulously arranged, half wet, half dry.

I'm on the set every day now. Elvis wants me to stay for the entire movie. I'm in. I'll probably fuck up my clientele at Sebring's, but I'm intensely curious about the whole moviemaking megillah and the people who do it. I have to take a risk. It's an easy program, I work like a makeup man—in between takes, I putz with Elvis' hair. Then I fade into the penumbra and observe the art and business of moviemaking. Few people even know that I'm there. I like it that way. The first thing I observe is, Elvis' Guys are always there. On the set, at home, living together, eating together. They're nice enough guys, but to be surrounded by this buttery bunch, on a daily basis? It's hard to believe that Elvis would waste his time and money on such a bullshit lifestyle.

A few days later, a bit actor in the movie asks me if I can trim one of his sideburns. As a favor, I do it. Twenty minutes later, as if his ass has been shot out of a cannon, the head of the makeup department shows up. The guy is steaming, wants to know what the hell I'm doing on the set when I'm not even in the union. He's sputtering like oil on a hot skillet. I'm trying to tell him that I'm with Elvis, but he's not listening to a word I'm saying. Fuck him. I walk away, go outside and smoke a doobie.

Within a few minutes, Joe Esposito joins me outside, wants to know what went down between the makeup maven and me. I lay out what went down and how the guy was screaming in my face and told me to get the hell off the set. Joe patiently listens, grins knowingly, says he will take care of the situation. Ten minutes later, reentering the stage, I catch sight of the makeup jerk quick-stepping to Elvis' trailer. He gives me a nasty squint. Within a few nanoseconds, he sheepishly emerges, his head bowed, and scurries off the set. I don't know what Elvis told him, but from now on I have the complete run of the set. Now everyone treats me with deference. I really do not like the feeling, except for the coffee and donut line in the morning.

"Shit. I'd never take that from him. Shit." Jim Kingsley is referring to Red West, the reigning bully of Elvis' Guys. Jim and I are in a secluded corner of the stage, witnessing a blatant display of Red's consummate bullying. Red grabs Gene Smith by the wrists and spins him like a top. Gene is yelping for Red to stop. Red ignores his pleas and keeps spinning. Finally he lets go, Gene bounces into a pathetic heap. That's when Jim says to me, "Shit, ah never take that shit from him."

Later in the day, I'm playing gin rummy (I occasionally step out of the shadows) with Alan Fortis, Richard "The Broom" Davis and Marty

Laker and, as usual, getting my ass raked over by these southern gents. I'm changing my mind about these southern guys. These guys are not dumb. Simple. But not dumb. Fact is, they're damn bright. Simple, but bright. Like I said, I'm having my ass raked over, when we hear a loud Kaboom! Kaboom!

"Say, huh? What's that shit?" mumbles The Broom.

"Gin." Alan proudly spreads his cards on the table. "See the winning hand."

"Damn, man. Sho, burned. Y'all beat my country ass," moans The Broom.

"Your skinny country ass gonna deal the cards?" asks Alan, his voice low and insistent.

"Howz about y'all let me win a hand?

"Mercy, deah Lawd, mercy," moans The Broom.

"Bout' ready to deal the cards?" asks Alan, his impatience peaking.

"I'm on it, my man. On it," says the Broom.

The Broom expertly shuffles the cards, Alan quickly cuts the deck. The Broom flicks the cards to us rueful players. For a moment, we seriously stare at our cards. The silence is shattered when we hear another Kaboom! Kaboom!

Now Elvis' clarion call resonates throughout the stage. "Somebody see what the hell is going on," barks the King.

The Guys snap to attention. "Right, boss," the Broom yells back. Then to us, "Sounds like it came from the red-light door" (the stage entrance, two doors in tandem, a cubicle in-between). The Guys rush to the door. For a moment, it's still…then the door slowly opens and Jim Kingsley quietly steps out of the cubicle. Doesn't say a word to anyone, save me, as he whispers, "I tol' y'all I'd never take shit from him."

So what went down was this. Red corners Jim in the cubicle. A right hook, a left jab, an uppercut, bada-bing, and Slim Jim knocks ol' Red on his ass.

～

I've just had lunch at a little taco stand on Melrose Avenue down the street from Paramount Studio. Now it's back to the stage. Shit, I forget the stage number. Anyhow, it's back to one of the stages. I roam around for a few minutes before I enter the right stage, then I take a real deep breath, preparing myself for what's inside—rampant egos, illusion, lies, winged dreams.

As I enter the cavernous stage, a strident bell clangs. Dead silence. Everyone, including myself, freezes in place. An authoritative voice bellows, "Take twenty-two. Acapulco!" Not a sound. No coughing, sneezing, nothing.

"Speed," says a softer voice (the director). Everyone hangs in place. "Action," says the director. I inch forward for a clearer view of the scene. Elvis is leaning casually against a creaky wooden fence. Three bad guys pop out of the bushes, grab Elvis and pin him against the fence. A camera quickly dollies for a closer shot. Quick as a well-oiled whip, Elvis springs into action. He surges forward powering the bad guys from their hold. They fall to the ground. Elvis breaks to the camera and with a half-sneer, half-smile, looks into the camera as it slowly dollies backward. "Cut! That's a take," declares the director.

As the crew prepares for the next setup, Elvis wastes no time in getting back to his dressing room. I seldom see him hanging around the set, except for the times he flaunts his karate prowess by breaking boards with his bare fists.

Someone is tapping me on the shoulder. I turn around. It's Alan. Alan is not a country boy. He's city all the way. A sterling sycophant, he's got that big bogus smile going when he wants something. He's having the time of his life traveling with Elvis. He's strictly along for the ride. I figure he has his own money, unlike the rest of the guys (save Joe Esposito) who scuffle along on the meager salary Elvis is paying them. About some things, Elvis is oblivious.

"Where y'all been? Elvis is waiting," asks Alan.

"There was a long line at the taco stand. So, what's up?"

"Elvis needs y'all to fix his hair. It's dipping in the back or something."

"I'm on my way."

Alan takes off his sunglasses and pans the area, making sure the coast is clear—then faces me and lays a big bullshit smile on me.

"What?" I ask him.

"Y'all got a couple extra of them loco-weed cigarettes?" he whispers confidentially.

"You're gonna get fucked up, man, go berserk, have to scrape you off the wall."

Alan's phoney smile hangs in there. "It's not for me. The girls go for that stuff." I tell Alan tomorrow I'll have a couple of joints for him. His bogus smile kicks up to high beam.

That little business taken care of, I head for Elvis' trailer. I feel absurdly sanguine today. It's a nice world. Things are much better than they used to be. I do a smooth slide to Elvis' dressing-room door. Inside the trailer, Elvis is running the electric shaver over his face as he restlessly paces the room. Charlie Hodge, Li'l Billy and The Broom are sitting in a corner of the room. I apologize to Elvis for not being around when I was needed. He's cool, says shit happens, forget it. He sinks into an overstuffed chair, surprised at its softness.

"I feel like li'l ol' Mickey Rooney in this thing." Elvis struggles out of the chair—resumes pacing. "All kinds of shit happening to me today. My moon must be in Pluto or Mars or San Diego or something. Weird-ass shit going down, man." Then over his shoulder, he asks Charlie, "Get everything done?"

"Yes sir. I surely have. Everythang is copacetic."

"Copa wha'? What the hell is that shit?" snaps Elvis.

"Burned," is Charlie's anemic reply.

"Copa bannas. Some ol' nightclub. Copa my ass."

Elvis turns to me in a different tone and asks, "You know about Red and Kingsley?"

"Yes I do."

Elvis lets go with a long sigh. "Ol' Jim. Ol' Red...Ol' Shep."

"Ol' who?" I ask Elvis.

"Ol' Shep, man. Some poor ol' fucked-up dumb-ass dog."

Charlie seizes the opportunity to join in with some down home levity.

"Dog's probably wandering 'round some ol' cornfield, corn so hot it's a poppin'," quips Charlie.

"Man, you sound like Julie Andrews or something," says Elvis.

"Hell no. Probably sniffing some ol' bitch," adds The Broom.

"Y'all think that ol' dog wants to wander around some distant cornfield, when he kin be sniffing a bitch?" says The Broom.

"Damn fool dog," says Elvis.

"Shoo, corn so hot it's a poppin', shoo, I never believe that stuff. Shoo, corn never git that hot in the field. No how. Corn a popping in the field. Dumb ol' guy," pipes Li'l Billy.

Elvis is chuckling. He gets a kick out of the country bantering, which he usually instigates. Now Elvis' expression changes, something has entered his mind. He vigorously shakes his hands and wiggles his fingers at his sides. The Guys pick up his vibe and clam up.

"Somebody wanna see me?" says Elvis, his voice low and level.

"The director 'n wardrobe," says The Broom quietly and a touch awkward.

"Tell the director I'll see him later. Tell everybody I'll see them all later. Tell 'em. Shit. Tell 'em something."

"Got it boss," says The Broom.

Elvis opens the dressing room door, peeks out, closes the door, wiggles his fingers and studies the makeup chair disapprovingly. Then reluctantly he flops onto the chair and faces the mirror. I jump into action. A couple of minutes into my routine, Elvis mumbles, "I made 'em shake hands afterwards."

"Hip," I mumble back.

"Man, that hadda be a luckly-ass punch."

"That counts."

"Red is bad, man, bad."

"So I've heard."

"I made 'em shake hands."

"Civilized."

"Man, I'm just trying to make a dumb-ass movie here. Shitty dumb-fuck songs. Dumb-ass director. My guys fighting on the set. Everything is copa, what the fuck!"

A pause. Everybody waits for the King to do whatever he's going to do. Elvis holds up his hands signaling for me to stop fussing with his hair. He stands up, the haircloth still draped around his shoulders.

"Anybody got a cigar?"

The Broom is on the job, he pops open an attache case, grabs a cigar, hands it to Elvis, Charlie flicks a Bic, and within two royal heartbeats the King is puffing and pondering. He unsnaps the chair cloth, it falls to the floor—and Li'l Billy quickly picks it up and hands it to me.

"Go on to the house," says Elvis to the Guys. The Guys are delighted now, save Li'l Billy. They can get to the girls they've been pitching on the set.

"Wanna Pepsi, Elvis?" asks Charlie.

"Nothing. Just get your copacetic ass out of here. And tell Sonny to wait in the car."

"Got it," says Charlie. The Guys split.

Elvis stares at his reflection in the mirror, sticks out his tongue, checks it out, then tosses his cigar into the sink. He heavy-eyes the makeup chair then, resigned, he solemnly sits. Once again, lickety-split, I toss the chair cloth over his shoulders. In mid-toss he bolts out of the chair. I'm standing there hanging on to the chair cloth like a misplaced matador. What am I supposed to do? Sit? Stand? Follow him around? What's on his mind? Is this another test for me?

A mini digression...

A couple of weeks ago I'm alone with Elvis in a studio bungalow. Elvis is in the kitchen. It's silent. Thump! Something hits the floor. What the hell is that? I rush into the kitchen to find Elvis flat on his back on the floor unconscious. I kneel beside him and pat his cheeks trying to revive him—what do I know? Nothing. Five nervous seconds slowly pass. Still nothing...I've got to get help. I'm about to sprint for the phone in the other room, when Elvis slowly opens his eyes, smiles, stands up as if nothing has happened. Later on in the day, Joe Esposito tells me that's one of Elvis' tests, to see how I would react if something had really happened to him. I guess I passed the test.

Where was I? Right. Now Elvis puts on his skipper's cap and walks out the door. I follow him. He wanders to the center of the stage and places his hands squarely onto to his slim hips and slowly scans the scene. Props, cables, facades...it's still, eerie. He spots a makeup table, stares at it for a moment, then slowly sits down, flips off his cap and tosses it aside.

"My hair, man," he says, pointing to his reflection in the mirror.

"Uh huh. Right," I mutter.

Okay. Once again, I lay out my hair stuff, flip the old chair cloth over his shoulder—Is he going to jump out of the chair? A short while later, I'm putting the final touches on the King's head. All the while he's been still and silent, staring at himself in the mirror. Then he starts singing "Ave Maria." Soft, serene, with a compelling sensitivity. For a few seconds, the ordinary has become sublime. This guy can croon a tune, for sure, for sure. He stops abruptly—His eyes are tearing...So are mine...

⌘

A couple months later, "Fun In Acapulco" is in the can. It's three o'clock in the morning. Ollie Hammond's on La Cienega Blvd. Jay and I are doing breakfast—we're rapping.

"I'm thinking about accepting Elvis' offer to travel with him. Be his personal hairdresser. What do you think?" I'm asking Jay.

"Just doing him?"

"Just him."

"To Memphis?"

"Says he has a nice place there. Plenty of room for me."

"Do it, man. It's gotta be trippy. Living in the King's Palace."

"Trippy. Let me tell you, man. There's some weird shit going on. And this fucked-up Colonel guy, his manager, is nuts. A control freako. He yells out orders like a drill sergeant. If he orders the Guys to bark and howl like dogs, they bark and howl like dogs. It's humiliating stuff to see, man." I can see that Jay is pulling away, into his own thoughts. I eat. I wait.

"It's been six months since Camy and I have split up."

I sip. I listen.

"I met this chick...She's something else. Beautiful."

"What's she into?"

"Actress. She's done a few things...She's gonna be a star, man. A fucking star. I can feel it."

"You smitten, man?"

"Huh? Smitten...? Maybe. But I still think about Camy."

"So, you're going through a choosing thing, right?"

"You cut to the core, man. Exacto!"

"What's her name?"

"Who?"

"Your new love."

"Sharon Tate...She's going to be big, man." Jay raises his cup of coffee to a toasting position. I join him. "To fame and fortune," says Jay.

"I'll toast to fortune. You can have that fame bullshit," I emphatically add.

I accept Elvis' offer to be his personal hairdresser, to do his hair exclusively.

CHAPTER THREE

This morning I'm at the King's place on Bellagio Drive, ready and anxious to go to Memphis. The Guys, all dressed in black one-piece jumpsuits, are busy loading the vehicles—a Rolls Royce, a station wagon and a customized Winnebago. I listen closer to their jabbering—I figure, amphetamine chatter—bucolic bunch. For the next few months I'll be spending a lot of time with these guys. I've become used to their parochial interpretations of just about everything in the universe. To them, I'm the "Hollywood" hairdresser. To Elvis, I'm still the "Holly-wood" hairdresser, but I sense, something else. I've yet to figure out what that something else is.

"Y'all got his sandwiches?" Jim Kingsley asks Alan.

"Y'all don't have them?" bemoans Alan.

"Damn. Shoo. He'll stretch our country asses from heah to Hong Kong," drawls Gene Smith.

"Shoo, how's he all gonna do that? Shoo," asks Li'l Billy.

"How? Shoo, that's simple. He'll stretch your ass, jes' like a chainling fence," says Gene.

Now Li'l Billy is getting all puffy. "Lookie heah, y'all talking out of ya haid. Jes' what the hell is a chainling fence? Talking like some ol' Chinaman! It's chain-link! Dumb ol fool," says Li'l Billy.

"Shoo, y'all know what I'm talkin' 'bout," giggles Gene. "I never know what the hell y'all talking 'bout. I 'spect some of that black-ass dye y'all put on ya haid done seeped through and into y'all's brain."

So it goes, the rustic banter, the confusion. But it's eyes front when Elvis emerges from the doorway. He's also attired in a black one-piece jumpsuit. He scans the scene, then reaches into his chest pocket, comes up with a long slender cigar and, with one deft movement, tears the cellophane from the cigar, crumbles it and tosses it over his shoulder. With noteworthy alacrity, The Broom lights Elvis' cigar.

"Trouble?" asks Elvis, his voice low and deliberate. In a beat, the Guys reply in concert, "No problems. Everything is ship shape."

"Everything is cool," blurts Li'l Billy.

Elvis turns around, gives Li'l Billy a long inquiring look. He can't help noticing how quickly Li'l Billy is picking up the big city lingo. Elvis is concerned about him (he's his blood kin) and watches him with a paternal eye. Elvis spots me standing on the sidelines. He motions for me to join him. "Want to ride in the Winnie with me?" he asks.

"Sounds good," I answer with a silly grin. The whole scene tickles my funny bone.

Once again, Elvis' eagle eyes swoop the scene. Satisfied that everything is accounted for and in a voice barely above a whisper, he says, "Hit it."

With much haste, the Guys scramble for their respective vehicles. Elvis climbs into the Winnebago, myself in tandem, followed by The Broom, Charlie, Alan and Joe Esposito. Elvis slowly lowers himself into the driver's seat and stares dumbfounded at the dashboard. My skin tightens. There is no doubt that this guy has a great talent, but driving a bus?

"How the hell do you start this big ol' doggy?" asks Elvis.

My face is red hot. Someone in the back of the Winnebago quips, "Y'all mean y'all cain't start her, boss?" Elvis turns to me for a reaction, now I see that it's a put-on. I smile and go along with the charade. Later on, Joe informs me that Elvis used to be a truck driver. I guess I feel better.

Our wheels hit the highway. San Bernadino, Albuquerque, Oklahoma City, Arkansas. Gin rummy, Pepsi Cola, uppers, candy bars. The deeper we get into the South, the more down-home the rapping becomes. Elvis tooling the Winnebago, chomping on a cigar, trading humorous lines with the Guys, all good natured sarcasm. However, you can only go so far with the King. If you cross the line, a strained expression crosses his face that says "Stop, go no further." Every once in awhile, Elvis calls out from behind the steering wheel, "Somebody get me a sandwich. And not with that weird-ass alfalfa hay shit in it either."

A chorus of "Right, E." from the Guys.

The Broom asks Charlie, Charlie looks at Alan, Alan looks at Joe— Joe points to a cardboard box. The Broom hands the box to Alan, Alan selects a sandwich, hands it to Elvis. Elvis has a couple of hasty bites of the sandwich and hands it back to Alan.

"Gotta Pepsi?" mumbles the King.

"Coming up, boss," sweet-talks Alan.

Once again, the Guys go through the same routine, locating a Pepsi for Elvis. Elvis downs the Pepsi in two masterful gulps. Revitalized, he cranks the Winnebago up to eighty miles per hour and motions for me to sit beside him.

Along the way we stop at nondescript motels, stay a night or two and then move on. More often than not, the proprietor never knows it was the King who stayed the night.

It's three o-clock in the morning—we're all sufficiently wired—somewhere in Arkansas. We pull into a remote roadside cafe. There's three or four customers inside the joint, a vintage jukebox playing a vintage tune, Hank Williams' "I Got A Feeling Called The Blues." A waitress with heavy mascara rambles to our table, looks us over, then turns and peers out the window at our impressive caravan of vehicles.

"Where y'all headed?" she asks.

Three guys at once. "Memphis."

"Bin ta Hollywood?" asks a local cowboy sipping a beer at the counter. Three guys at once. "Yes sir."

"Figures," says the cowboy.

"Musicians?" asks the waitress.

"Kinda," mumbles Gene Smith.

We give her our order: junk, French fries, cheeseburgers, Pepsis. We dive in. The usual wisecracking chatter. I'm getting used to these country boys.

A few minutes later, a squeaky door opens and in ambles Elvis. What a pity things like this don't happen more often. Everything stops. Every atom comes to a screeching halt. All eyes on the King. It's fascinating and loony at the same time. (Come on, it's gotta be an awful way to live.) The waitress' face flushes with surprise. She blathers breathlessly, "Y'all him? Y'all really him?"

"Yes ma'am, as far as I know. I'm him," Elvis politely answers, his lips curled in an impish grin.

"Can I have y'all's autograph?" pleads the waitress. In a half a second she comes up with a pen and paper. Elvis scratches an autograph and gives her a kiss on the cheek. She swoons. For a moment I thought she was going to collapse. That done, Elvis gives the high-sign for me to join him outside. I can see that he's in no mood to play the "Star."

Outside, it's a warm, clear night. An occasional semi-truck blasts past eating up the highway. I spot Elvis gazing at the full moon, his hands placed precisely on his slender hips. I crunch across the gravel driveway and join him. What's going on? Did I fuck up? Am I through? What? Elvis, his back to me, is staring at the moon. For a couple of minutes he's mute, then slowly and deliberately he says, "We're getting close to Memphis, Sal."

"Wonderful. I'm looking forward to it."

"Man, it's nothing like L.A."

"I need a change."

Glancing over Elvis' shoulder, I spot the gaping waitress — her nose tightly pressed against the cafe window pane, her eyes straining for a glimpse of the King.

"Everything alright?" asks Elvis.

"Everything is fine."

"Need anything? How 'bout the Guys?"

"Cool." Elvis is wholly aware that I have no desire to become part of the Memphis Mafia gang.

"If you need anything, talk to Joe."

"Thank you."

Elvis does a slow turnaround and faces me. He's about to speak, he hesitates, looks me over..."I still have the country in me...with all the show business stuff, the studio...I'm known all over the world, man. Everybody knows 'bout me...Eskimos know 'bout my ass. Some ol' mountaintop in Tibet, they know 'bout me...Famous, man...It's hard to hold on to your roots with all that shit happening, man."

"I hear you."

"I'm from the country. I don't want to lose that part of me. I keep the guys around me. Keeps me from falling into the star-world. I'm a singer, man. That's what I am. I'm best at that. That's what I gotta do. I love to sing, man."

"I have to cop out. I don't know anything about your songs, except maybe 'Hound Dog' and a couple of others."

Elvis smiles, says nothing — looks up to the cloudless sky. "Man, shit's going on. Everything is twinkling up there. Something is going down. Things are happening."

I go with it — nod my head.

Elvis points his forefinger at the boundless universe. "That shit up there didn't just happen."

"Right. Things seem to be rolling right along," I affirmatively add.

Indicating the sky, he continues, "Something, someone, got all this shit together."

"All beings are flowers blooming in a blooming universe."

"Say, huh?"

"Zen. I'm into it."

"Zen?"

"We are all one. Stuff like that."

"You believe in God?"

Damn, I don't know how to respond to that question. For the last couple of hundred miles I've been sitting beside Elvis while he drives. All the time he's been rapping nonstop about the bible and shit, I've been listening, not saying much. It's all cliche thinking. What the hell do I say? Should I say, don't get excited? Tell him the bible is a myth written metaphorically years after Jesus' death? He'd ask what does metaphorically mean? So then I gotta tell him the meaning of the word. That's exactly what I'm not into. Now I become the smart-ass guy from Hollywood. This guy is living the life of the chosen few, the exalted, the superhuman. He should be telling me what metaphorically means.

My answer is vague and noncommittal. Elvis gives me a long ineffable look. Then as if on cue, we both turn around and head for the van.

Standing alongside the van are two teenage girls. They see Elvis and scream with unabated ecstasy.

"My Lord! It's you! It really is you!"

"My Lord!" echoes the other.

Joe squeaks open the screen door and calls to the girls. "That's right, ladies, it's Elvis. But please don't scream about it, I have enough troubles."

Elvis asks the girls if they would like to ride along with him in the van for awhile. The girls shriek joyously. Everyone is instructed to watch their language and manners. No funny stuff with the girls. Have a few sandwiches, a soda pop, sing a few songs—everything pure and pious.

A few hours later we stop in one of the many mini-towns along the way. Elvis buys the girls return bus tickets. Joe stuffs a few bucks into their pockets. The girls are totally transfixed, giggling and crying at the same time. In a matter of minutes the locals get wind that Elvis is in town. Bam! At least forty people gather around the van ogling the King. For the next half-hour Elvis signs autographs and poses for photos with them. He waits until everyone gets a peek at him, then we finally leave.

Jesus, I could never live like that. It's crazy. I mean, why would anyone want to live like that? These people are hypnotized. There is a constant input of impressions, knowledge and energies received in our heads, hands and stomachs. It's everywhere, even in a cup of tea. It goes on and on. Very sadly few will ever grasp it.

Later, when our slow-moving caravan rolls across the Tennessee state line, someone shouts, "Graceland!"

"What's Graceland?" I ask Joe.

"His house," whispers Joe into my curious ear.

"You're kidding? Name a house?"

Joe shrugs his shoulders and grins.

CHAPTER FOUR

We arrive at Graceland at two in the morning. About forty people are faithfully planted at the front gate of the mansion. "Fans?" I ask Joe.

"Fans," he intones.

"How did they know Elvis was coming?"

"They're here all the time."

"You're kidding?"

"You'll get used to it."

We drive past a sentry post, in front of which a gnarly-looking guard waves us on. Up a winding driveway we go, leading to a plantation-style mansion. Inside, Elvis insists on giving me a personal tour of Graceland. It's blatantly obvious the King is not into matters of interior decorating. Garish, overdressed, the place looks like a brothel. After a few minutes, Elvis loses interest in the tour and motions for Joe to complete the task. Elvis skitters up the stairs.

"What's that all about?" I ask Jim Kingsley.

"His girlfriend. Priscilla," whispers Jim. Elvis never mentioned Priscilla to me. I'm curious.

"Come on, I'll show you your room," says Joe, indicating for me to follow him downstairs. There's a pool table, a soda fountain, an adjacent room filled with the King's gold records hanging on the walls, and finally a bedroom with a queen-size bed, onto which I immediately flop totally exhausted. Now I'm wondering if I'm doing the right thing, working for the King. I could never ladle out the phoney sincerity at which the Memphis Mafia are remarkably adept. I'm discovering that the King is an acutely complex person. His awesome talent has not come easily. He's paying a price. I wonder if he knows it?

For the few days I stick around the house. The cook, a sweet black lady, is sincerely anxious to feed me, but I cannot get into the Southern fare. I haven't seen Elvis since we arrived. He's been upstairs in his room locked up with Priscilla. I hang out in the Golden Album Room. Its low ceiling is bordered by indirect lighting. In the center of the ceiling

dangles a satellite chandelier complete with sparkling lights. A faded
pink sofa curls halfway around the room. In front of the sofa, there's a
low-slung, shiny-black coffee table on top of which a large plastic bird of
paradise mutely squats. Opposite the sofa is a hefty reclining vinyl chair
that slips out from under you when you sit on it. There's also a big screen
television and a state-of-the-art sound system—my headquarters. After
three days of being voicelessly planted in the recliner chair gazing at the
TV and listening to country and rock music, Charlie informs me that
the King is ready for my services.

Okay. Now I sashay upstairs to the King's inner sanctum. I'm
introduced to Priscilla. I'm startled. She looks about fifteen years old.
She can't be much older. A glassy adolescent stare, a ho-hum body, a
painted piece of cake. What the hell does the King get out of her?
Methinks, she's more of a possession than a person to Elvis. His virgin
baby doll? Hey, who the hell am I to judge? Right? Still, I never figured
that the King was into a kiddy-bag thing. My image of superstars and
how they live is rapidly evaporating. I re-remind myself that I'm an
observer.

It's a tranquil day. I'm puffing and jogging around the Graceland
grounds. I haven't seen Elvis for a couple of days. He's been locked up
in his bedroom with Priscilla. So I'm jogging. I don't know what the hell
else to do.

Save Jim Kingsley or Charlie Hodge, the rest of the gang stay at
their own places during the day, then dribble by in the early evening, at
which time Joe Esposito briefs us with the latest bulletin. Is the King
getting up? Does he want to do something? Midnight movies? Roller-
skating? Amusement Park? (He rents the entire park for himself.) Hang
around Graceland? Buy clothes? (He rents the entire store for himself.)
Get his hair done? That's me. That's where I come in.

If the King needs my humble services, I'm here. If not, I'm free
to take off and do whatever I want. Thing is—save the music—there's
not a hell of a lot to do in Memphis. Joe Esposito tells me that I can use
one of Elvis' cars if I wish. I respectably decline the offer. I like to move
unnoticed, but that's impossible. Everyone in Memphis recognizes
Elvis' vehicles, from the Pink Cadillac down to the garbage truck. They
smile and wave, do the "thumbs-up" thing. One might as well wear a
neon vest blinking, "I'm with the King." I much prefer to call a cab and
worm around town sub rosa. That way, it's real.

I'm in the gold album room, playing on one of Elvis' guitars. It's a quiet night. That happens occasionally. There's no one in the mansion except for the cook, Elvis, Charlie and myself. Elvis slips into the room, skipper's hat on, black shirt and trousers, black wrist bands. He's toting a couple of books, puffing on a cigar, and holding a big glass of ice-cubed water. He asks me how I like the guitar. "Fine," I reply. Then he asks if I wouldn't mind if he joined me? "Delighted," I delightedly answer.

Right about now, I get a bit flummoxed. What kind of bag is he into tonight? What's the social matrix this evening? The parameters of speech and content? See what the hell I put myself through? It's not like talking with a close friend. Although at times it can be just that—tight, connecting. It's when we get into the cosmic stuff when the tight thing happens. But little stuff, and he gets all blown out.

Last night at the Memphian Theater, we saw "Lilies Of The Field" starring Sidney Poitier. After the movie, in the limo on the way back to Graceland, a couple of the Guys and Elvis are having a discussion about the movie. After a few minutes, Elvis asks me what I think the movie is all about. I offer a pithy reply, which happens to be the antithesis of his opinion of the movie. Bam! A titanium door slams in my face, with a sign that says "Do Not Enter." In giving my opinion I've undermined his, and that don't cut it with the King. I've since learned that I can't be that open with him when the Guys are around. When we're alone it's a different thing. Anyhow, he doesn't talk to me for two days.

Elvis settles down on the pink sofa, hands me the books he's carrying and says, "Some things on karate."

"Thanks, I'll check 'em out."

"How's everything going?"

"Good. Real good, man."

Elvis sniffs the room. "Been smoking?" he asks.

"Absolutely."

"Be cool, man."

"Always."

Elvis has a sip and a puff on his cigar, then eyes me. "Sal, you ever take LSD?"

"Absolutely. Yes." I place the guitar aside and sit across from Elvis waiting for him to speak.

"I've read some on it."

"Reading about LSD is nothing," I say.

"Nothing?"

"Well, it helps a little, I suppose. But reading about it is like eating the menu and not the food."

"Damn."

"LSD is not something to chippy with, man. If you take it in the wrong surrounding, with the wrong people, it can flip you out. Little story here. One time I took acid when I was at Jay's house."

"Jay Sebring?"

"Right. Jay and I are friends. So I drop the acid and head for the bathroom to make water."

"To do what?"

"To urinate."

"Damn."

"In less than five minutes, the acid kicks in like a bazooka. I leap for the mirror to see what my face looks like. Here's the thing, it's a three-way mirror, like a clothing-store thing. Now I'm checking out my image in three mirrors at once. In one mirror, it's the man. In another, it's the teenager. In the third mirror, it's the seven-year old boy. Now the images are looking at each other, checking each other out."

"Damn. What happened?"

"Everything! God. Where did that innocent kid go? What happened to him? And the teenager and the fully grown man? Then I'm happy, then sad, then I'm crying. Three hours in the bathroom. Finally I force myself to pull away from the mirrors and go downstairs to the living room. I hang my head low, ashamed to let anyone see my face, then they would know that I'm a complete nut. But that was not the case, everyone else was going through their own trips, paying no attention to mine."

"Anything else?"

"Well, it goes on. The oneness hits you heavy. We are all one. The whole shot is one. It's the feeling, more than that, it's the not knowing that hits you."

"Not knowing?

"Yeah. Then you know."

"Damn."

"Dig it. I looked at my hands as if they belonged to someone else. I mean, who the hell is that someone else? Anyhow, man, that's some of the LSD trip."

"How about the hereafter?"

"The who?"

"The afterlife?"

"The same question was asked of a Zen master. Is there life after death."

"Uh huh," mumbles Elvis. "So what's his answer?"

"How should I know, I'm alive!"

"Damn." Elvis is sweating. Reaching for a nearby box of Kleenex, he wipes his clammy forehead. Druggy pills are taking effect. Uppers? Downers? Both? His mind swerves into another direction. He slowly pans the room, eyes the shiny albums adorning the walls. "Damn," he says, like he's amazed at what he sees.

"What's that, man?"

"I started with a li'l bitty guitar. 'Bout this big." He spreads his index finger and thumb a couple of inches.

"That's bitty, man," I confer.

We silently sip our drinks, his water, my wine. I sense that this is not one of the nights where the weight of the world is on his shoulders. He picks up the guitar, strums an E chord. He acts surprised. "Thing's in tune. I heard you playing. Sounds good. I know a couple of chords, I play the shit out of them."

Another strum. Then he eases into "Red Sails In The Sunset," his voice clear and sensitive. I sit back and listen. This is a special moment for me. Here I an alone with the King, kicking back on a pink sofa listening to him singing to me. After the final strains of the tune, he has a sip of water, then eases into "Are You Lonesome Tonight?" After singing a couple more soulful songs, he says if I need anything to ask Joe. Then sets the guitar aside and leaves.

Fourth of July. Elvis orders a truckload of fireworks. The Guys slip into asbestos suits like warriors, then the battle begins, shooting fireworks at each other inside the house. Curtains catch fire, rugs smolder, lamps topple, furniture is upturned, sparks flying all over the place, crazy shit happening. On slow days, when the madness ebbs, the Guys give him bogus awards for his karate prowess or for his ability as a football player or some other silly-ass bullshit thing.

A few nights later, it's ten o'clock and I'm in the King's bathroom dyeing his hair—jet black—he's intensely silent. What's wrong? Now he's staring at his fingers. There's definitely something on his mind. I wait...He turns to me and pointedly asks, "You believe in reincarnation, Sal?"

Shit, what do I say? How do I handle his ontological curiosity? Shall I tell him about the great metaphysical and spiritual teachers of this world that address these kinds of curiosities? Do I pile up a bunch of words? I gotta go the shortcut way, with a pinch of Zen.

"No."

"Why not?"

"Reincarnation deals with time. Time, as we know it, is an illusion."

"How about being born, then dying? An illusion?"

"A fantasy."

"Shit, man, wha'chu saying?"

"Everything is an appearance. Mingling forms and energies. Am I a form? A spirit? Is there a God? These questions don't mean shit," I pungently reply.

Now the bathroom becomes glacial and as still as a tomb. Have I gone too far? You have to watch what you say to the King, lest it displease him and pitch him into a dark mood. Was I arrogant, pompous? After a few minutes of awkward silence he sighs, then picks up his electric shaver and runs it over his face. His eyes survey me. He's studying my every move. A full five minutes roll by before he clicks off the buzzing shaver and carefully places it on the floor. Then he lowers his head and covers his face with his hands.

"Sho-biz. Bizzzzzz. Bizzzzzz. Sho Bizzzzzz," he solemnly incants, pinching the tip of his nose.

"Nitrogen, nitrogen. Niii-tro-gen. Niiiiiitroooooogennnnn. Nitrogen. Nitrogen. Niiiiitrooooginnnn."

His words become a mesmerizing drone.

"Shhhhhhoooooobizzzzzz. Shobiz. Sho. Sho. Sho-biz. Biz biz. Shooooooobiiiiizzzzzzzz."

He cups his fingers over his nose.

"Niiiiitroooooogiiiiiinnnnn! Nitrogen Bizzzzzz. Bizzzzzz. Bizzzzzz."

He stops, looks up at the ceiling as if listening to a voice.

"It's here, man. Receive it. Receive. It's here. All of it! Here. Life is here, full of crazy jive." Elvis looks around the room, his eyes widen, he grins. "It's here. All here. The light. The light is here." Now he becomes less certain. "To receive is no longer in this world? Can I receive and still stay here? Can't ah stay?"

He grabs his chest as if stabbed in the heart. What follows are varying expressions of sorrow, indignation, anxiety, horror and amazement.

"Shit. Ah, ah, shit. Ah, ah, ah, fuck. Damn! Oblivion. Damn."

Elvis fiddles around searching for a particular TV tape. He finds it, inserts it into the tape gizmo, presses a button—nothing. He mumbles some shit about science fucking up your head, then presses a few more buttons, stands back and waits for something to happen. Yow! The blaring sound bounces off the walls. Elvis jumps for the volume control button, turns it off. Now the tape starts rolling. I see that it's newsreel footage of General MacArthur's farewell speech to Congress. While the tape is spinning rapidly forward, Elvis turns to me, looks me straight in the eye.

"Old soldiers never die. Never die. No dying. No dying today, Mommie. Not today. Never die. Old soldiers never die."

He pokes his finger at himself in the mirror.

"Never die. Y'all got that, man? Never happen. Old fuckin' soldiers never die. Never happen."

He looks up to heaven.

"Never happen. I'm spreading the light. Getting it on. Ah' got the vision and the action. Ah' got the action. Who?"

Elvis waits for a reply from the void—from the terrible silence which fills him with the suspicion that he could be going mad.

"Who? Who? Old soldiers never die."

He laughs, low and diabolical. He salutes the whirling tape. Then it dawns on him to stop the tape, however, it's not the scene he's looking for. He presses another button, the tape spins forward.

"Old cat jes' faded away. Faded out. Jes' faded out, way out. Way out. Ol' corncob turned to dust. Faded his ass away. Great, man. Faded out."

He talks to his mirrored image.

"That ol' general did a lot for this country. They didn't fuck with him in those dark shades and that ol' pipe. He said he'd be back and the man came back, strutting off the li'l ol' landing barge, walking right into the water. Right up to his knees. Shoes on and he's walking in the water. Don't mean shit. Always get somebody to shine his shoes."

Elvis starts singing "Git offa my blue suede shoes," then resumes his stream of consciousness.

❧

"Some ol' private always around to shine the general's shoes. Cat has style. A warrior, a motherfuckin' warrior. A King. Shit, I'm a King too. Right there (pointing to the commode in the bathroom), that's where I sit. That's the throne. Ah, the general."

Elvis fiddles around with the gizmo's buttons, finally the TV screen fills with MacArthur's image delivering his farewell speech to the United States Congress. Elvis clears his throat preparing himself for a speech. He shuts off the TV.

"Ah have jes' left your fighting sons in Korea. They have met all tests of—uh—shit, fuck."

He pulls a cigar out of his shirt pocket, searches for a lighter, finds one, lights up, has a few cogent puffs while thinking about what he's about to recite. I can feel his wheels spinning. He steps to the center of the room and bows as if addressing an audience. He pauses, looks at the audience waiting for their complete attention.

"Ah'v jes' left your fighting sons in Korea. They have met all the tests there, and ah can report to you without reservation, they are splendid in every way."

He clears his throat. Pauses for effect.

"It was my constant effort to preserve them and end this savage conflict honorably, and with the least loss and a minimum sacrifice of life. Its growing bloodshed has caused me the deepest anguish and anxiety. Those gallant men will remain often in my thoughts and in my prayers. Always."

He scans the room with melodramatic sincerity.

"Ah'm closing my fifty-two years of military service. When ah joined the army, even before the turn of century, it was the fulfillment of all my boyish hopes and dreams."

He spreads his arms wide.

"But ah still remember the refrain of one of the most popular barrack ballads of that day, which proclaim most proudly."

Now he pauses, lowers his arms and takes a deep breath.

"Ol' soldiers never die, they just fade away. And like the ol' soldier of the ballad, ah now close my military career and jes' fade away. An ol' soldier who tried to do his duty as God gave him the right to see that duty."

He bows humbly to the "audience," makes a "V" for victory sign with his fingers and throws kisses into the air. He then goes to the small refrigerator and extracts a bottle of Perrier, swills proudly from the bottle and belches.

"God gave him the light to see that duty, and he faded his ass away. That was his duty, to fade his ass away."

He then breaks into a song.

"One for the money, two for the show, three to get ready and go, cat, go! Git your fucked up feet off my blue suede shoes. Uh, uh, I'm all fucked up. Yeah yeah. Uh, uh right."

As quickly as he began to sing, he stops.

"Words, man. Words. Words all lined up, nice and neat. Millions of words all lined up one after the other. Like soldiers. Big ones, small ones.

He closes his eyes and stands still, his arms hanging at his side. Then he breaks out in full voice, a la Mario Lanza.

"Because God made you mine. Pope's hopes, twinkle-dinkle-wrinkle Rip Van Wrinkle. Count down, count up, count sideways, count backwards, equal rights, equal wrongs, without a song."

He stops singing, has a swig of Perrier water. He poses defiantly, with one hip thrust forward, and speaks to the mirror.

"Cosmic power. Power. Power. Divine power. Cosmic power!"

He looks up at the ceiling, the floor, his hands. He digs his fingernails deeply into his pasty white arms. He raises his voice as if speaking to a jury.

"Do y'all want to hear my case? I ain't the blame for everything! Some motherfucker gonna listen to my case? I see. I see...I fuckin' see."

He's trying to convince himself of something. Something beyond this reality? He flops down onto the chair. Covers his face with his hands. He sinks deeper into the chair, becomes still—closes his eyes and feigns snoring...After a couple of minutes, his eyes pop open. Now he feigns disorientation.

"Huh, Wha'?"

He sighs, takes a deep breath, twitches his fingers and shakes his hands as if he doesn't know what to do with them. He speaks to my mirrored reflection.

"Book of the dead. Look at the dead. Hair on my head. Far east. Far out. Christ masters. Secrets. Thump, thump, mother ship, father ship, baby ship, space ship."

He springs out of the chair and wiggles his legs.

"Whole lotta shaking goin' on. Shanties, panties, FBI, getting high. Take one, take two."

He attempts to mount the TV set.

"Fans, cans—take one, take two. Take me. Shake me. Ice cream, mess kit, mess cat, army, heil Hitler, barracks hair, eardrums, back fuzz. The shroud over my head? Nitrogen. Niiiitrrrrroooogeeeeen! Niiiiiitrooooooooogen."

He presses his face tight against the mirror—he breathes hard, fogging up the mirror, then draws a happy face with his nose. He has an almost incestuous intimacy with forces that can crush and maim you. The look on his face. He remembers all. The way his father had tended him, the way his mother has tended him. His mind is wide open, he races forward, spontaneously exploring his deepest thinking.

"When I was a child, I spoke as a child. But when I became a man, I put away childish things...Bullshit. I'll always be a child."

For a moment, it's silent. He sticks a cigar in his mouth—searches for a light, to no avail. He looks at me. I shake my head no. He flips the unlit cigar into the bathroom sink. His bleary eyes canvas the bathroom, then he gives me a big chummy smile. I can dig where he's coming from. I smile back.

CHAPTER FIVE

A few nights later, I'm taking my nightly stroll around the Graceland grounds. The air is still, the bright moon is full. I spot Elvis sitting alone on the back porch. This is a rare moment to observe Elvis away from his predictable minion. He looks around as if he hears something. Nothing. He buries his face deep in his palmed hands and sobs. Intimate sobs...I'm thinking about a Kenneth Patchen line that says, "Lonely is a bad place to be."

It's Christmas time. The snow is piled high, giving Graceland a distant and muted feeling. I'm rapidly approaching ennui. I need to touch and feel passionate flesh. I ask Elvis for a two week furlough. He's most gracious—blesses me and, within two hours, I'm on my way back to the City of the Angeles, back to Marilyn.

The first couple of days in Los Angeles, I'm into some serious fornicating, locked up in Marilyn's apartment in West Hollywood. West Hollywood is—save the music—the complete opposite of Memphis. Art galleries, bookstores, fine restaurants, theater—all the city stuff right at your fingertips. For me, it's home and I'm delighted to be here.

After my errant libido simmers down a taste, I give Jay a call. He sounds genuinely pleased to hear from me. Says he's going on a house call, would I like to tag along? Two hours later, I'm sitting beside Jay in his spiffy, shiny blue Cobra sports car, slinking through Beverly Hills. Jay is diligently scanning the scene, eyeballing the beautiful broads strolling along the posh sidewalks, all looking like magnificent birds.

"Chickadees," remarks Jay, "Chickadees."

We continue rolling along, panning the scrumptious scene...I'm sensing something is on his mind. After a few minutes of eye-straining activity, Jay turns to me.

"You know what's happening?" he asks.

"No, what's happening?"

"Chicks, man, fucking up my head."

"So, what else is new?"

"Camy," says Jay, his voice low and sad. "We split up, man."

"You want to get back together?"

"Shit, I don't know. I've been digging this one lady, man, she's got me tripping."

"This the actress you told me about?"

"Yeah, Sharon Tate. She's a fox, man. I want you to meet her. She speaks fluent Italian too."

"Sounds like a love trip. You in love?"

"Do I know?" Jay is quiet for a moment. He checks his image in the rearview mirror, finger-combs his hair—adjusts his shirt collar.

"Whaddaya think, man?" I tactfully ask.

"I think we're going to be late for Lump Lump."

"Say wha'?"

"Lump Lump, man. Red Skelton."

"'The' Red Skelton?"

"The one and only. Ol' Willy Lump Lump." Jay gooses the feisty Cobra and we spring to Jack Entratta's condo in Beverly Hills.

Jay introduces me to Mr. Entratta (Jack is the owner of the Sands Hotel in Las Vegas). He's a big guy, early fifties, smooth, cordial—says to call him Jack. I can live with that. Jack excuses himself and leaves the room to fetch Mr. Red Skelton—Lump Lump. Jay and I are alone in the living room. Jay is unconsciously clicking his tongue, a thing he does when he's anxious. He looks at me and makes a clowny funny face. I hear chuckling. Enter Jack, Mr. Skelton, and one beautiful broad, about fifty. Looks like an ex-showgirl thing going on. I'm trying to be cool, but I'm flashing.

Ol' Lump Lump looks like a sedated hermaphrodite—soft and gooey—as if his entire muscle system has collapsed. With Jack's assistance, he moves in slow motion, like he's swimming in a pool of jelly. He faces me and stares with glassy unfocused eyes, while Jack does the intros. She's Mrs. Red Skelton, he's Mr. Red Skelton. I got it.

Lump Lump lays a staccato "hello" on me, then inches his way into the kitchen. We silently follow him. He checks out the kitchen. Runs his hand over the refrigerator, tap-taps the sink, stares vacantly at the kitchen table for a moment or two...then turns to us, smiles and snails-out of the kitchen, Jack and Mrs. Skelton hot on his tail. Coming from the living room, Jay and I can hear them going through a heavy discussion trying to decide where to cut his hair.

"He's gotta find the right vibe, man," whispers Jay.

"The right vibe?"

"Yeah. The vibe. Gotta have it."

"Is this a Carlos Castaneda thing—the Brujo—Don Juan—on the front porch telling what's his name to feel the vibe and that's where to sit and all?"

"Yeah, that's it. The vibe. Man."

"Heavy shit going down, man. How long do you think it will take?"

"Wha'?"

"For the man to locate the vibe. How long?"

"Never know. A few minutes, a few hours."

"A few hours! Jesus, man, I gotta a busy karma goin' on, gotta catch up on a few things, life is zipping by, here I am in a unused kitchen—loitering."

Jay covers his mouth with his hand smothering a giggle. One look at him and you guessed it, I'm doing the same. We chill and wait for the jabbering seance in the living room to fade. After a few moments, Mr. Skelton (I shouldn't call him Lump Lump. I'm not disrespectful of the man. He has a tragic aura around him. Like all great Comics? Comedians? A person whose behavior elicits laughter?) slowly pads back into the kitchen, Jack and Mrs. Skelton attentively on either side of him. He gazes at the kitchen table for a full two minutes, mutters something incomprehensible to himself, sighs, and finally sits on top of the kitchen table. Is this it? Are we ready to roll?

Mr. Skelton smiles and starts telling us a corny joke about a farmer and his dog. We're on! Jay whips the chair cloth over Mr. Skelton's sagging shoulders, bada-bing, Jay gets right to work. Now, Mr. Skelton is giggling "hee hee" when he delivers the punch line to a really dumb joke. Jack and Mrs. Skelton bogusly laugh along with him.

Meanwhile, Jay is feverishly snipping and clipping his rusty locks. Jay combs Mr. Skelton's hair forward, covering his forehead—it's gotta be a foot long. Snip! The hair hits the floor with a dull plop. The room freezes. It's absolutely an inglorious moment. Mr. Skelton stares unbelievingly at his severed clump of defunct hair neatly piled on the aseptic kitchen floor. He's whimpering like a constipated infant and toddling like a three-legged turtle. He splits to the bathroom from which we hear a stream of intensely lucid and graphic expletives affirming his unequivocal disapproval of the "whacko" thing that Jay just did to his hair. I'm saying he was pissed. Big time pissed.

Pandemonium. I mime to Jay that I'm splitting. He tosses me the keys to the Cobra.

I'm sitting in the Cobra waiting for Jay. Fifteen minutes later, he pops out of the building, skips and dances down a few steps Fred

Astaire-style—then smoothly slides to the Cobra, slips behind the wheel, adjusts his Gucci driving gloves and asks, "Wanna eat, man?"

I nod yes.

"Mexican?"

Another nod.

"El Coyote?"

Another nod.

We screech and peel away from the curb and merge into the busy afternoon traffic. I'm waiting for Jay to tell me what went down with Ol' Willy Lump Lump (damn I shouldn't say that). Jay's face flushes, he's holding back a laugh. "Well?" I inquire.

"It's one of those unfortunate things, man. I was just informed that Red uses the long-hair-in-front thing as a prop for several of his characters. So when I whacked the thing off, it kinda fucked up his act. I was just informed."

"Big time info."

"Jesus, man, you should've seen them. They were running around in circles bumping into each other, trying to cool the cat down." Jay can't hold back any longer. He bursts out laughing. In three seconds, I'm laughing with him.

A few days later, it's back to Memphis. Back to the King's castle. It's almost noon. I have a throbbing headache, my body aches, my scalp feels itchy—I feel crummy. I've been up all night rapping with the King about the cosmos and shit. Last night we got into the resurrection and it's true meaning—the mythological religiosity behind the whole three-day trip and what went down with the big "J" popping up and him saying howdy to the folks hovering over his cold dead ass. I'm saying the resurrection is a continuing event. In Christian terms, we move from the small life into the great life. The life in Christ. In universal terms—the life that is the "I Am," that we all are. He's checking out the viewpoints. I'm spouting like I know what the hell I'm talking about. I mean we're both stoned out of our heads—I gotta say what I believe, at least be closer to the truth. Whatever that is.

I'm about to dump my weary body onto my satin-sheeted bed for a few hours of urgently needed hibernation. It seems like two seconds before I'm abruptly awakened by the shaking hand of Jim Kingsley. "Time to go," he barks in my ear.

"Got it. Up, up and away," I wearily respond.

"We're leaving in a few minutes."

"Leaving? Where?"

"Nashville. A recording session."

"I thought that was next week?"

"Elvis changed his mind. It's today."

In the living room above, I can hear the Guys chattering like a squad of nervous squirrels. "What's all that about?"

"The Winnebago isn't working. So Elvis got a bus for the trip."

"A bus. Did he buy it? Rent it?"

"I suspect, one or the other."

A few minutes later, I join the guys huddled around the front door of Graceland checking out a big shiny Greyhound-sized bus planted in the driveway. After a few minutes of the usual banal banter I hear, "Let's hit it." The King is ready to roll. One-piece black jumpsuit, black boots, black gloves, black wristbands, sunglasses, skipper's hat, the whole magalia. The King is grinning. He feels good. Wonderful. I'm in no mood for a bad mood.

In no time we're gayly motoring down the highway heading straight for Nashville. I'm sitting beside Elvis. He's driving the bus—puffing on a stogie, sipping on a Pepsi, and mumbling all kinds of off-the-wall stuff. I'm semi-freaking out. The man is not paying as much attention to his driving as I think he should. He's not looking at the road ahead of him as much as I think he should.

"Get myself to Nashville. Resurrect my ass," Elvis firmly declares.

"Uh-huh," I croak, my bloodshot eyes glued to the highway.

"Resurrect the musician's asses too. And anybody else's ass that need resurrecting."

"Nothing to it," I squeak, my burning gaze ever steady on the highway traffic ahead.

"Shit, man, you look like you could use some resurrecting yourself," says Elvis looking at me.

"I'm cool," I lie.

"Hungry?"

"No. Thanks. No. Not hungry."

"Damn. I need somethin'."

That said, Elvis lets go of the steering wheel, stands up and nonchalantly heads for the back of the bus, like the monster is on automatic pilot or something.

I freeze.

Allen Fortis—who has been sitting behind Elvis—lunges for the vacant steering wheel, grabs it and plops into the driver's seat. Now we're bouncing along the shoulder of the highway—pebbles, holes, brush, we don't miss a thing. Finally we pounce back onto the highway. Allen regains control of the behemoth bus. I'm forever grateful for his timely alacrity. From the rear of the bus, Elvis and the Guys are laughing their asses off. I've been had. It's a ploy—a setup. Another one of Elvis' put-ons. One never knows when he's going to do it. The Guys are used to the routine—however, this time Allen didn't move quite fast enough, hence the bouncy thing on the highway shoulder. Like I said, the King is in a good mood.

For the first few days in Nashville, everybody is up. Feeling good. It's a party. Sleep during the day, up at night, do Elvis' hair, go to the recording studio. It's trippy watching Elvis doing his "thing." The man has elephant ears. In two minutes, he's got the tune down. His musical instincts are finely honed. He has an intense concentration while still being at ease. The deeper he gets into the music, the more he unveils himself. He gets "down to what it is." The musicians respect him. They should, he's an artist. But, very unfortunately, the songs he's singing are pure shit.

By midweek, the whole scene is totally mirthless. Dreary. Elvis is pissed—he hates the stupid songs he has to sing for the movie. He's pissed and if he's pissed, the Guys are pissed too. Me, I'm bored and depressed. I'm losing money every day playing gin rummy with the Guys—I'm wired, shaky and sleepy.

Hooray! Joe Esposito tells me that we're going back to Los Angeles to do another movie. Man, just in time. I'm longing to get back to the city—back to my own lusterless life.

The movie is called "Kissing Cousins." It's a three-week location shooting at Big Bear mountain resort, about a hundred miles from Los Angeles. In the movie, Elvis plays a dual role—one character is a backwoods country boy, the other a sophisticated Air Force pilot who comes to visit his country cousin. Elvis wears a blond wig for the country boy role. Everything is done in triple time.

In between takes, I remove a wig, under which Elvis' hair lays flatter that a Louisiana pancake, then with much haste I miraculously (like Elvis says) resurrect the mother for the next scene. Elvis hates the movie, despises playing the hillbilly role and singing the dumb-ass songs.

It's midwinter, freezing weather. Cold icy wind. Not my bag. However, there are a bunch of female extras in the movie scantily attired in simple mini-country frocks. Bare feet and bouncy bosoms abound. So that's kinda neat. That's positive, but I'm still freezing.

The hotels in town are filled to capacity. Elvis knows I'm not into doubling up with anyone, so he rents an entire off-season lodge for little ol' moi. The lodge is located on the lakeshore. Big place, about forty rooms, all the furniture covered in black drop cloths, even in the bar. Eerie. For an hour or so, I'm going around in circles checking the place out. I'm driving myself crazy trying to decide which room to choose. Eventually I settle on a small, cozy-warm room with a panoramic view of the lake. My home for the next few weeks.

It's now been two weeks of shooting, most of which is done near and around Big Bear Lake. Today they're shooting about a hundred feet away from the lodge—my lodge—where I'm sitting on the front porch, legs propped onto the railing observing the tricky metamorphosis of moviemaking. Lunch break. The actors and crew make a beeline for the catering trucks. For a moment, reflectors, ropes, cables and cameras dominate the scene. It's tranquil, reflective. I'm slipping into the "nowness" of my existence. I'm euphoric...

Shit, I hear Colonel Tom Parker, Elvis' manager, shouting out orders to the Guys. He's a powerful deal maker in showbiz. His real name is Andreas Corelial Van Kulikk, who's an illegal immigrant from Holland. He's been a dogcatcher, pet funeral director, carnival barker, concert promoter, manager for Hank Snow, ta da ta da. He's got Elvis under his greedy thumb, always one step ahead of his world famous client. I read him as a egomaniacal, illiterate martinet pumping out all kinds of bullshit. Around him the Guys are like limp puppets waiting to have their obsequious strings pulled. One vociferous command from him and the Guys do all kinds of humiliating things. He tells me I should be a hypnotist. More bullshit. One day I ask him how he got into show business?

"Chickens," is his quick reply.

"Chickens?" I echo.

"Yep. Folks come from all over town to see them chickens dancing."

"Dancing chickens?" I really have no desire to engage this man in conversation, but my innate curiosity takes over. Okay. I'll play the straight man. "Tell me, sir, how do you train a chicken to dance?"

"Simple. I put a couple of chickens on a countertop. Underneath the countertop, I have a grill. I turn on the grill, the countertop gets hot. I put a couple of chickens onto the countertop and the chickens start to dancing."

"Brilliant," I say duly impressed by his wizardry.

Right now I hear him shouting and growling like a drill sergeant to the Guys. "Everything alright, boys?"

"Yes sir, Colonel sir!" they reply in chorus.

"Any problems?"

"No sir, Colonel sir!" they dutifully respond.

"Let me hear you bark like dogs."

"Yes sir, Colonel sir!"

What follows is a concert of canine howls and barks. Man, this Colonel guy is one wacky fuck. Why the hell the Guys put up with his bullshit is a major mystery to me. I have to remind myself that I am but a vigilant observer of the "Hollywood Scene."

Two frigid weeks creep by. I'm cold. When I'm not doing the hair-thing for Elvis, I'm in my cozy room reading or gazing at TV. Save a few evenings of undiluted lust with one of the hillbilly pussy-posse extras in the movie, the monotony on the mountain is getting to me.

There have been a couple of cast and crew parties at a local hotel banquet room. Fifty or sixty people—the usual party din. Peppy music, showbiz-speak, clinking ice-cubed glasses, etc. In a far corner of the room, Elvis, looking like a svelte maharishi, holds court flanked by two of his Guys and a typical flock of fans riveted to his every word and gesture. Elvis eats all that bullshit up. Or at least he pretends to. I don't know. With me, he's completely different. He knows that I know it's all bullshit. Maybe that's part of the bond, I think, we have between us.

It's early in the morning. Elvis, Joe Esposito and I climb into the Winnebago ready to head for Los Angeles. I'm anxious to split from this freezing-ass cold location and get back to the city. I haven't had a decent plate of pasta in three weeks and I have an urgent need to laugh hard with someone—someone like Marilyn Brown. Elvis slides behind the wheel, he puffs on a cigar, tugs at his wristbands, adjusts his skipper's cap. Joe sits alongside Elvis and I'm sitting behind Joe at a small pull-down table. Elvis is telling us how happy he is that we're finally leaving the dumb-ass movie location. He cranks up the Winnie, sparks his stogie, and we follow a lead car driven by one of the Guys.

"Damn, I need to get away from this north pole shit. Pine needles sticking to my country ass. Damn ol' hound dog (referring to a hound dog in the movie). Big ol' droopy eyes staring at me. Reminds me of the ol' days. Big ol' ears. Breath like an alligator. Damn ol' dog...How 'bout you, Sal, you have enough of this place?"

"Indeed I have. Take me back to civilization. I'm ready," I joyfully reply.

"Dumb-ass songs. Singing to some dumb ol' hound dog." Elvis is percolating right along in his ranting. Suddenly he's silent. His eyes are riveted to the road, his hands tight around the steering wheel, his face taut and pale. I look out the window and observe that we are on a steep and narrow stretch of road, with a sheer drop of several thousand feet. I also realize that we are picking up speed. Right. I'm peering out the window now. Faster and faster goes the Winnebago. Right. We are rapidly descending a mountain on a narrow road. Right. Faster and faster. Too fast.

Okay. This is one of Elvis' little games to scare me. I'm wise to his act. This time I'm not going for it. Faster and faster. I look at Elvis. He's in a cold sweat—biting hard on his cigar. Man, this is real, he's not acting. "What's happening!" I yelp.

"Brakes just went out!" cries Elvis over his famous shoulder.

"Wha' the fuck?. Who wha'?!" I'm blurting.

Now Joe gets into it. "Easy. Easy. The rocks. Watch the rocks," he says guiding the King's driving. "Right—more to the right. More. Left. Left. Watch it!"

I'm nailed to the window, peering in horror at rough and jagged rocks protruding from the mountainside. This is no put-on, this is serious stuff. We're veering toward the edge of the mountainside and we just missed a car in front of us by mere inches. Joe and I wave frantically at one of our cars trailing us to pull alongside and, above the brattling grind of the transmission, we yell, "Clear the road, the brakes just went out!" Peeping through my spread fingers, I woefully glimpse at the traffic in front of us racing frantically to get out of our way.

"The sides. Watch the sides. The edge! The edge! Watch it," reiterates Joe in a strained voice. Now stuff in the Winnebago is shaking, breaking and falling. "Ease up. Christ! Watch it!" cries Joe on the verge of panic.

Reality smothers me like a heavy blanket. My Sicilian blood takes over. "Let me out of this thing," I cry, bolting for the door.

"Sit down," snaps Elvis as he desperately downshifts while scraping the side of the mountain with the side of the Winnebago, trying to slow it down.

"You know how this will read in the newspapers?" I shout. "The headlines will say, 'Elvis Presley Dies In Mountain Road Accident' and somewhere in little bitty print it will mention my name. Man, if I'm going to die, I want equal billing!"

Jesus Christ. What a stupid thing to say. Dumb. Dumb. My feeble attempt in dealing with panic. Stupid. Dumb. Maybe he didn't hear me. Who am I kidding? He heard me. Elvis ignores my emotional outburst, being as he's super busy struggling with the errant Winnebago. Luckily, we hit a stretch of level road. Elvis rides the Winnie to a bumpy stop. I'm out of the thing in half a second, thankful to be alive. Joe is right behind me. Elvis? A stiff silence. Finally he sticks his head out of the Winnie—he gives me a long hard glare. That's it. I blew the gig. It's over. I give him a silly grin back. I feel I should be kicking gravel with my toe. Now the Guys pull up and join us. I'm wondering where I can have my shears sharpened for my next gig.

Elvis shakes his hands at his sides, a sure sign of frustration. In a whisper he says, "Equal billing?"

A heavy pause. Everyone looks at Elvis...

"Equal billing?" he repeats.

Elvis tells the Guys what I blurted when we were swerving and scraping down the mountain. Now everyone is laughing, including me. I learned that Elvis is as skillful a driver as I have ever seen. He handled the out-of-control vehicle with remarkable calm.

Elvis and I, circa 1962

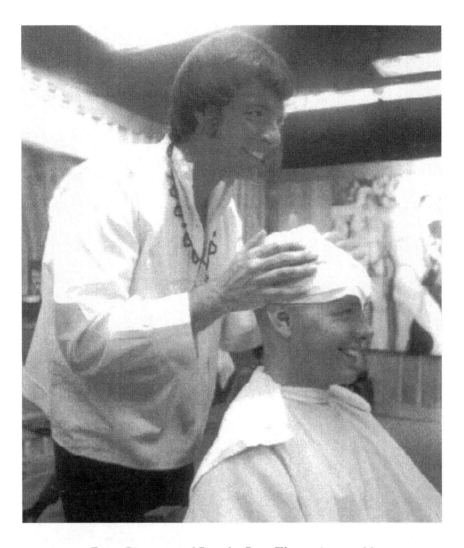

Russ Giguere and I at the Iron Flute, circa 1966

Sam Cooke and I, circa 1961

Jay Sebring and I, circa 1964

Graceland, circa 1952

Some of the Memphis Mafia, circa 1962: Jim Kingsly, George Kline, Joe Esposito, Marty Lacker & Richard (The Broom) Davis; Elvis' father in background

Vernon Presley (Elvis' father), circa 1963

Graceland, soda fountain, circa 1962

Golden Album room, circa 1962

Elvis and I, circa 1962

CHAPTER SIX

I'm running through life's many vicissitudes like a mouse on a treadmill. This is a good time in my life. Hell of a good time. Feeling good—frisky. I'm with Marilyn, my dream girl. We've been together for a year. So far, no negative bullshit. We share many mutual interests and curiosities: books, music, movies, painting, frequent sex, stuff like that. One more really vital thing, she's not afraid to laugh, and she makes me laugh.

Elvis lays a stack of martial art books on me. One of the books is about a guy named Oyama. He kills bulls with one punch to the heart. Man, I'm not into that. It's the eye and hand coordination and the mental centering it takes to do it that interests me. I tell Jay what's happening with the karate trip. His eyes light up—he's interested. I've learned that when Jay gets interested in something, he goes balls-out.

For the next few weeks, we see every martial arts flick in town. We eat sushi—that didn't work out too well—we mimic the Samurai sword movements. Before you can say "Toshiro Mifune," Jay arranges for us to take private karate lessons at his house. Our instructor is Ed Parker, a big powerful Hawaiian. When Ed arrived for our first lesson, Jay and I and Jay's gigantic dog (don't ask me what kind) are kicked back at the poolside. Ed waves to us as he comes down the stone steps leading to the pool. The monster canine eyes him. He growls deep and throaty, then takes off running. He viciously pounces on Ed, snapping and growling. Ed twists and turns avoiding the dog's huge jaws. Jay swiftly subdues the dog and chains him to a post. "Man, holy fuck. Sorry 'bout that," says Jay stroking the dog.

"That's okay," says Ed calmly.

"He was just trying to protect me. You look like trouble to him."

"I understand."

"You alright?"

"I'm fine."

"Sorry, man."

"It's over. Let's get to it."

We head for the house—I spot a trickle of blood on Ed's arm and there's a tear in the seat of his pants. This guy could have snapped the dog's neck if he wanted to, yet he was absolutely composed while the dog was trying to bite a chunk out of his ass. He doesn't seem ruffled at all. I'm duly impressed. I believe I've just had my first lesson in the martial arts.

For the next few months, the routine is, once a week Ed comes to Jay's house and instructs us for a hour or so, after which the three of us have breakfast cooked and served by Jay's valet/chauffeur/cook. Joe's his name. He rarely says a word and never gets in your way. (I figure he's a part-time junkie with some jail time behind him. Jay helps out all kinds of people.) After breakfast, Ed splits. Jay and I drop a touch of LSD and review our lesson, followed by some spirited sparring.

Okay, let's zip ahead a few weeks. Jay and I are in the Cobra, descending Benedict Canyon, heading to Sunset Blvd. We've just finished a karate lesson from Ed at Vic Damon's house. Vic turns out to be a super guy—mannerly, soft spoken. He has a place set up for us to do the karate thing in his backyard behind the swimming pool. Vic says he wants to learn some up-close moves to protect himself because, in his world, fights usually happen in crowded bars or rooms. Could Ed teach him some moves he could use in such a situation? Ed assures him that he can. For the next hour, Ed shows us a panoply of punches and blocks with Chinese names like foo hung, chow pop, bing bang—which I'm sure Ed made up on the spot.

After an hour of moderately vigorous instruction, breakfast is served by a worker bee (a youthful Latina lady) on a long table covered with a white tablecloth and starchy-white placemats. Cantaloupe, eggs benedict, nothing wrong with the fare. We eat, we split. Vic escorts us to the Cobra, we do the goodbyes and we're gone. Ol' Vic is alright. Good pipes too.

Now we're on Sunset Blvd. This street has the "Hollywood vibe" down. I'm marvelling. Just over the hill, there I was hunkered down in the Valley—another world. Like I was on Neptune or Pluto. Jay has been rattling on about Sharon Tate and how he thinks it's love, but there's this film director, some guy named Roman Polanski, to whom she's presently engaged and that's kinda fucking up the whole scene. I'm half listening to what he's saying. I mean, Jay has so much stuff going on in his life, if I were to listen to all of it, I would be completely exhausted. Still, I've got to tell him something. I really don't want to, but I've got to.

"How's your new pad?" Jay asks.

"You picked up my vibe, man."

"So?"

"It's on Sweetzer Street, right off Melrose. It's nice. English country thing going on...Fish pond...Quiet. Man, you will not believe who has moved in right next door to me."

"Cary Grant."

"Close. Get this...Camy."

Jay's face turns pale and tight like a brand new kettle drum. We abruptly screech into a sharp swerve across two lanes of traffic, a few more dazzling maneuvers—bibity-bip—and we're illegally parked on a side street. Jay switches off the purring Cobra. He looks straight ahead at nothing, lets out a long wheezy sigh. "My Camy?"

"None other."

"Goddamn. You know we're estranged."

"I know."

"We're still married. Legally, we are still married. You know?"

"I know."

Jay cracks his knuckles and ponders the situation. "Has she seen you?"

"No. Not yet."

"Good, good. Make sure she doesn't see you, okay?"

"You're the boss."

Jay checks out his teeth in the rearview mirror. I can tell that he's orchestrating some sort of plan. "Beautiful, man. Beautiful."

It took two days for Jay to persuade me to assist him in planting a microphone in Camy's apartment. Tonight, Camy splits for the evening. The plan is on. I phone Jay. Forty-five minutes later, Jay is discreetly tapping on my apartment door. Lugging a substantial suitcase in each hand, he grins as he noiselessly slips into my pad.

"Jesus, man. What's all this?" I'm referring to the suitcases.

Jay opens the suitcases and spreads their contents on the floor. Several mini-microphones, tape recorder, voice-actuated devices, earphones, Ninja outfits, black tennis shoes, black scarfs, gloves, the whole shot. "Whatcha think, man?" asks Jay.

"I thought it was going to be a couple of things. Man, this is heavy. I mean, what are we doing? Why all this stuff?"

"It's kicky, man."

Jay settles down on the sofa, fishes in his side pocket, comes up with a small pipe, stuffs the pipe with a ball of hash, matches the pipe, has a long pull, hands the pipe to me.

"Kicky, man," Jay repeats.

"Kicky? It's breaking and entering. Plus invasion of privacy, plus, who the hell knows what?"

Half an hour and two pipes later, we're donned in regulation Ninja attire. Then we ever so surreptitiously creep and crawl silently into the night. Miraculously, we make it to Camy's apartment door unseen. "Dig this gizmo, man," Jay whispers.

He fools around with the lock for a few seconds with a snappy wiry gadget made to do such illicit things. The door swings open. Dauntless, he eases into her apartment, my sweaty self in tandem. I maintain vigil at the front door while he does his thing. Clicking on his nifty Ninja flashlight, he silently pit-a-pats through the apartment planting several concealed mini-mikes throughout. Like I said, I'm sweaty. What the hell am I doing here? Life is never dull with Jay. That's why I'm here. At the moment I don't feel villainous, only stupid.

After ten acutely apprehensive minutes, what with folks flowing in and out of their apartments and Jay's Ninja flashlight, the light of which bounces off the walls and can easily be spotted half-a-block away, we're done. We splito.

The next night, Jay, forever stealthy, shows up at my apartment lugging yet another suitcase of electronic paraphernalia, which he promptly sets up in my bedroom. He hangs around, we watch TV until one o'clock in the morning. Finally, Camy arrives with some guy. Jay perks up and gets with the program. "Earphones."

I hand him the earphones, which he carefully places onto his morbidly curious head.

"Both of them are in the kitchen."

"Wonderful," I whisper.

"It's quiet. I think they're kissing."

"Right."

"That's gotta be it. Kissing."

"Gotta be."

"The bedroom...In bed...Kissing and messing...She's giving the guy head. I can tell. She slurps a lot."

"Man, this is primal stuff. Why do it?" I ask. Before Jay can answer, I beat him to it. "I know, it's kicky."

That's how it goes for the next week. Jay sneaks into my apartment, catches the daily "broadcast" for a couple of hours, then we zip to Canters Restaurant on Fairfax Avenue for a late night nosh, during which he prattles on about Camy and Sharon Tate and how he's hung up on Sharon. But there's Camy and he thinks he loves her too and that's another thing and, man, at the end of the day, I'm drained. I've had enough, I tell Jay to get the stuff out of my apartment or I'll do it myself.

"Of course, my man," he replies, playfully pinching my cheek, "Tomorrow night."

"We skip the Ninja thing, right?"

"But (mimicking Count Dracula) of course...So what's with the King?"

"Man, I don't know where to start with that trip. He's Lear in your face. Tragic, ironic, paradoxical, ambiguous, contradictory, the whole shot. What gets me is the awe. Whatever time of day, wherever he's standing or sitting or yawning, people stare unabashedly, their mouths agape, salivating with serious awe. It's fucked up, man. Way up. It's embarrassing to be around that kind of silly dumb-ass bullshit."

"What's he into?"

"Narcissistic. Big time. He's demanding, incredibly sensitive. Schizoid, textbook stuff, kind, gentle. A man. A boy. A King. Just all kinds of shit going on, man."

"You like him?"

"Yeah, I do. He has an innate sense of honor and he can be humorous as hell."

Jay leans in close to me. We lock eyes. "Thanks for putting up with my spying trip."

"You're never boring, Jason, but you've got to watch that edgy shit."

"It's all a game, man. A game," says Jay, his eyes bright and shiny. "Tomorrow, after I take the stuff out of your apartment, then I'd like you and Marilyn to meet Sharon."

"Sounds good."

"Seven, seven-thirty, dinner."

"Wonderful."

The next night, snaking up Jay's twisty driveway, Marilyn informs me that Sharon Tate is a rising star and how beautiful she is and a fine actress and whatever. I'm half listening—I'm expecting the usual typically-gorgeous Hollywood broad, doing the typically-phoney showbiz bullshit. Look at me. Aren't I stunning? I'm incredible. My hair, teeth, skin, I'm fucking perfection. I know, I'm ranting.

Man, was I wrong. Sharon is lovely, unpretentious, personable, humorous, intelligent, all capped with a primal sexuality. After a tasty dinner prepared and served by Jay's houseman, Joe, the four of us settle down in the living room. Jay has some really fine ganja, we get into that, add a few brandies, before you know it, we're having a hell of a good time. Not once in the entire evening did we talk about showbiz.

CHAPTER SEVEN

Plink, plank, plunk, rat-tat-tat, whomp, honk, clink—Elvis at the helm of the Winnebago, playing the Winnie like a musical instrument. Drum-riffing on the dashboard, the floorboard, the sides of the vehicle—clinking, tapping, honking. All this happening while he obsessively sings the title tune of the movie he is about to make, "Viva Las Vegas."

I'm sitting beside him—we, me and a couple of the Guys are on the highway heading for Vegas. We're about a hundred miles away from "Sin City," it's hot and sticky—we're all wired to the eyebrows. Elvis has been singing and resinging the title song of the movie since we left Los Angeles. Over and over, a mesmerizing mantra. "Bright light city gonna set my soul, gonna set my soul on fire. Viva Las Vegas, Viva Las Vegas!" Banging, clinking, tapping. "Viva Las Vegas, Viva Las Vegas!"

Jesus! It's gotta be the nine-hundredth time he's belted out the tune, I'm getting meshugeneh listening to it. Elvis is buzzing like a hungry horsefly. He's a joking, laughing, singing fool who doesn't give a shit. The vibe is supercharged, a lot different from the molasses-slow "Kissing Cousins" scene. The man is moving with rocket-propelled energy. Why? Why do it? All that running around from one place to another. Make a movie. Sing a few songs. More running around? What kind of a life is this to live? Why? Money? I know. I know. There are copious reasons for having money. Money begets money. I know. Why am I here? Money. I'm guilty. Let's leave it at that for the moment. Okay. It's a high. Let's face it. Elvis loves to get high too. Super fucked-up high. Is that why he does it? Shit, I don't know what the hell I'm saying. This is the kind of dumb shit one thinks about when one is also wired to the brow.

We're billeting at the Hilton International Hotel. Snazzy. I've been here for two weeks. The City is writhing with energy. Everywhere you go—a restaurant, supermarket, car wash—you hear, "Elvis is in town." The guy walks on starlit water. Each stage show we attend, the performers pay tribute to Elvis. They unfailingly announce that Elvis

Presley is in the audience, the spotlight swings to Elvis, he waves, smiles and mumbles, "Get the damn light out of my face," and sits down. When the King is present, the performers push themselves to the top of their talents.

I don't know how he does it. Everywhere he goes, people pathetically swoon, their desperate fingers longing to touch him. It's revolting. I got a taste of the madness a few nights ago when Elvis, a few of the Guys and moi went to see Clara Ward and her gospel singers appearing at one of the hotels on the Strip. As is customary, hotel security was prepared ahead for his Kingly arrival. Our entourage enters the hotel lobby. I'm a few steps ahead of Elvis. A nearsighted old lady—gotta be eighty—mistakes me for the King. She pounces on me like a hungry jackal onto a rodent and starts screaming "Here he is! Here he is!" as she's tugging at my jacket. "No, no, no! I'm not Elvis. No. Really, lady, you got the wrong guy," I urgently inform her. She's not listening. She waves to a ravenous pack of fans behind her. "Here he is!" she yells. In a beat, a gaggle of fanatics form a tight circle around me. I'm done for. This is just what I need. A bunch of whackos wanting a piece of my jockey shorts. Very fortunately, Sonny West breaks through the mob and diplomatically deescalates the situation. "Jes' go on in a' see the show, folks. Elvis will see y'all later on."

After pulling myself together in the men's room, I rejoin Elvis and the Guys in the hotel's showroom. Naturally, we have a primo table. The show is about to begin. Elvis looks wistfully at me, then his face broadens into a lopsided smile. He pats me on the shoulder and asks, "How'd you like it?"

"No thank you. No way."

"Man, that li'l ol' lady was gone," quips the King.

"She sure was. I was hoping Sonny would get to me a lot quicker then he did."

"Next time," whispers Elvis.

"Next time?" I'm about to pursue the subject further, when drums roll, lights dim, music starts, the show begins. I learned an important lesson that night. Stay way behind Elvis and the Guys. Unnoticed, untouched.

❧

It's been three weeks of hurry, wait, go, stop—my interest in the magic of moviemaking is beginning to fray. Save a few times of lust-making with one of the extras on the film, I'm ready to go home. It's six o'clock in the morning, it's sweltering hot. I'm in the royal bathroom, attending to Elvis' hair for the day's shoot as he skillfully glides an electric shaver over his boyish face while listening to a cassette tape of Eddie Arnold singing "Make The World Go Away." He's chewing up the song, digesting every word, every syllable of the tune. "Damn. That's true. True. Shit's true," he mutters to himself, finding new layers of meaning to the words. I'm dyeing his hair coal black, while digging his contrapuntal rap to the song.

"The man is laying down some powerful words. All kinds of shit happening in the world everyday. Nighttime too. Everyday, everywhere, shit's happening. The country is all fucked up. Hell, the city is fucked up. Hell the world is all fucked up." Suddenly he bellows, "Make the fucking world go away!" I'm startled, I accidentally topple a bottle of hair dye onto the porous sink and countertop, staining the fine Italian marble. Elvis, still singing, takes one look at the messed-up marble, then a look at my chagrined expression and breaks out laughing. I'm all apologies.

"Man, that kinda shit don't mean a thing."

I'm down with that.

"It's a whole lot better than that ol' top of the cold-ass Kissin' Cousin's mountain," says Elvis.

"What's better?"

"Huh? Las Vegas. Lot better."

"Yeah, I'm not into that cold number."

"Polar bears, seals, Eskimos. Freezing."

"Hell with that."

"You sweating, Sal?"

"It's hot already."

Elvis hold up his index finger, a sign for me to stop whatever I'm doing. He rewinds the audiotape to the beginning of the same song. Once again, Mr. Arnold's deep twangy voice sings proclaiming, "Make the world go away, take it off of my shoulders."

"Wha'cha think, Sal?"

"The world thing?"

"Wha'cha think?"

"The long or short version?"

"The pithy version." That's a word Elvis picked up from me last week. He's been saying the word every time we talk.

"A bit of pith it shall be. The universe, which includes the earth, is working perfectly, says Taoism. Isn't that interesting?"

"Damn, man. You mean all the shit we go through in life is perfect?"

"The world of opposites. Can't have good without evil. Up without down, in without out, here without there."

"Stop, go. On, off. Happy, sad. Shit, damn, let the world go away— but not today," the King sings concluding.

Later on in the day, we're in the desert shooting exteriors. A hard-hot rain has just pummeled the desert floor. It's gotta be a hundred and eighty degrees—I'm spent and gooey. It's been a wild ride on a surreal merry-go-round. I've seen most of the shows in town with Elvis and the Guys. Okay, there's an plethora of female extras in the movie. Okay, I'm getting laid. Okay, I've gambled away all my money, and my salary for the next six months is already gone. Okay, I'm depressed. It's like I'm in a halfway house, between the movie world and the real world. My self-pitying muse is abruptly cut by an authoritative if not petulant voice. "Hey, are you Elvis' hairdresser?"

Wiping the salty sweat from my eyes, I focus and recognize the diminutive figure of Paul Anka (my musician friends tell me that he's a real asshole).

"Yes I am," I lilt.

"I need a haircut."

"Really."

"Can you do it?"

"No sir."

"No? Why not?"

"I only do Elvis' hair."

"Only Elvis?" he says, stiff-necked.

"Yes sir, that is correct." I can see that he's not at all happy with my answers.

"I'm Paul Anka," he proudly proclaims.

"Yes sir. You are."

"Jay Sebring cuts my hair."

"None finer. You can't go wrong," I retort with a forced smile.

"You mean, you won't cut my hair?" He's getting miffy now.

"Yes sir. That is correct." Mr. Anka walks off in a huff. My friends were right.

I step back into my shady spot and catch up on my own dilemmas. Ten minutes later, Joe Esposito joins me in a cool lean against the prop truck...

"I just spoke to Paul Anka," say Joe rather wearily.

"Did I fuck up?"

"He said that you told him you only do Elvis?"

"That's what I said. Did I fuck up or what?" I catch a faint smile in the corner of Joe's mouth.

"I have to tell Elvis what happened."

A few minutes later, Elvis sticks his head out of his dressing room trailer door and motions for me to join him. I join the King in his deep-freeze trailer. Elvis said I can stay in his trailer anytime I wish, but I never do. I need my space too.

"Joe says that Paul Anka asked you for a haircut and you told him no?" says Elvis, his voice soft and low.

"I told him that I just do you, man."

Elvis has a sip of Pepsi, breaks into a delighted grin. "Whad he say?"

"Nothing really. He wasn't too happy. Looked like he lost his thunder."

"Pulled ol' Paul's Anka, huh?"

"Anka's away. Or some shit." We split a damn good laugh.

A couple of nights later, I'm doing my usual thing—losing money at the crap table—when I hear my name being paged over the casino P.A. system. Not the usual anglicized version, for once it's properly pronounced. "Ore-reh-fee-cheh. I check it out. It's Jay, and he's with Harry Cohn, Jr. (son of the movie mogul producer). I'm invited to join them at the Rivera Hotel.

The dreamy tones of Billy Daniel's ripple through the Rivera lounge. I'm with Jay and Harry at the bar (Harry's cool, a no-bullshit guy).

"How ya' doing, man," asks Jay leaning over his margarita.

"Yeah, I know, I look like shit," I reply.

"You lost weight."

"I'm walking around like a zombie. This town is freaky."

"Freako..."

"Everybody is amped."

"Freako."

"Wired to the eyebrows. Then, there's the King and his supernatural trip. Man, it truly wears one down. A study in illusion, maya, whatever. Wherever he goes, whatever he does, the sea parts, like he has his own personal cosmology going on, man. Then, the nutty people."

"Fans."

"Right, whatever they are, climbing over each other like starving puppies for a peek at the guy. That's when I feel cut off from the human species. We're all vibrating in the big 'OM,' man. Sometimes I forget that, but it becomes painfully clear at those ridiculous moments."

"You like him, man?"

"You can't help but like the guy. He has a certain sense of the untouched,"

"Innocence," injects Jay.

"Exactly. But I'm saying, he's into a heavy pill trip, man."

"Uppers?" asks Jay.

"Uppers, downers, sideways, he's got it covered, banging his brain, man, like he's trying to destroy himself."

"Needs help?"

"Yes. Absolutely. He's gonna grind himself to dust the way it's going. Thing is, everyone tells him he's fine, perfect. No one really talks straight to him. Tell him to fucking cool it, or to seek a psychiatrist pronto."

"How about you?"

"Like what, man?"

"You talk straight to him?"

"You speared me on that one. That's another thing. I bounce back and forth on that one. Drives me pazo. Jesus, man, there's so much shit goin' on. The guy is an industry unto himself. What he's done and what he's doing, is why he is, what he is, and where he is, he's the uber Kahuna of the universe. All that bullshit is goin' down, man. Hard to get through all that, man, and still keep the gig. Answer to your question—Do I talk straight to him? As much as I can. I'm a realist. I'm not here to be his Mind-Maven. I'm here to do his hair."

"Is that what you tell yourself?"

"Dumb. I know."

"You're a Changeling. You were meant to be in his life and his in yours. That's gotta be it. Far out, man. Sounds like I got here just in time. Look, man, your tight with—probably the most famous man on the planet. All kinda shit has to be going down with that kinda action. How about Sonny West?"

"Sonny and Joe are cool. Joe runs the whole show. He practically controls the hotel when the King is there. I've never seen him blow his cool with people. Sonny is a genuine gentleman. A credit to the South... Enough with my trip. What's going on with you, man?"

"I'm here to do Jack Entratta and Anka."

My face feels hot and red. Jay catches it.

"Whad I say?"

I tell Jay what went down with ol' Paul and the hair thing, and me saying that I only do Elvis and blah blah. Jay laughs at the whole scene, says I'm going to be a star.

A couple of drinks later, Jay, me and Harry (who hasn't said a word), traverse the hotel's buzzing casino and head for the main showroom. Once inside the crowded showroom we're guided to a ringside table. We sit, trumpets blare, the curtain slowly raises. I'm wondering, who is the performer? Out comes ol' Paul Anka! Jay is into a serious giggle. Paul dribbles out a couple of less-than-mediocre tunes, he spots our table, comes over to say "hi" to Jay, sees me and sheepishly smiles and shrugs his shoulders. Maybe he's not such a complete asshole after all.

ᴖ

I'm kicking back in the King's air-conditioned trailer. I've just finished re-dyeing his hair for the next scene in the movie. Outside the comfort of the trailer lies the steamy-hot Nevada desert. All kinds of action is going on: fume spewing, thundering motorcycles, screaming racecars, actors, extras, gaffers, makeup artists, the whole scene melting like a Dali clock. I definitely need a rest before I rejoin the surreal scene. Elvis sits and faces me. He's puffing on a long skinny cigar and sipping a Pepsi. He sighs and looks me dead in the eye.

"Sal, this show business shit can do crazy things to a man."

I evoke a feeble, "Yeah."

"Sal, you know I want both of them." (He's talking about Ann Margaret and Priscilla). "Which one? What do you think?"

He's smitten, big time smitten. I can dig it. Ann is a knockout broad. Beautiful, cheerful, talented, sexy—not too deep (he likes it that way). Ann is always ready to play games with Elvis—motorcycle riding, skeet shooting, chewing gum—whatever the King is into, she's right there with him. In vivid contrast, Priscilla is picture perfect. Hair, lips, eyes, fingernails, teeth, shoes, dress, perfection. Priscilla is callow and static. Ann is not. Priscilla is dull. Ann is not. Priscilla is not yet a woman. Ann is all woman. Do I care? These are my impressions—don't mean shit. True, maybe it's not a bull's-eye, but I'm not that wide off the mark. Lately I find myself right in the middle of the King's romantic dilemma, trying to figure out what he should do. He does that—opens his world to me. I never know what the hell to say. Say the wrong thing and he goes into a blue funk for days. Yet he wants it straight and honest...I give the man a velvet stroke.

"Do the East coast, West coast thing," I discreetly suggest.

"The what?"

"East coast, West coast. One here, one there. Can't go wrong, man. What the hell."

"Man, you been smoking that shit again."

His vacillation between Ann Margaret and Priscilla, I don't think is serious. He's above it all, hovering, looking down on the mundane scene. The implied smile, the silent grin. He knows the game well. Now, it's obeying him—that is the phenomenon—makes him an explorer. It absorbs his attention. Is there a prophecy? The explorer stirs. He's pissing on his own grave. My conclusions, unsystematically assembled and in part, I'm sure, misunderstood, will evoke incredulity with the public spin. His is a complicated mind. Someone's got to wander into its vastness and give it justice. Who? His phony friends? The Guys? I guess it's me. I make no defense, I'm not a psychiatrist, I've simply thrown myself into his world. In so doing, I'm discovering more than I want to know. He clings to the "Elvis thing," and anyone who gets in his way is a possible traitor. While his loyal fans peacefully munch on "Big Macs," the King is suffering and struggling over Ann versus Priscilla.

Meanwhile, he cleaves his way through the multitude of his fans— if he can reach the open he can fly. Elvis looks hard at me for a second, then breaks out laughing. "Sal, this business can mess you up."

The same conversation has been going on for about a month. Which one? Ann or Priscilla? One a woman, one a child. The man has a wide range. From board-breaking machismo to a baby-talking eight-year-old. Traveling with him, on occasion, we have had adjacent rooms. Through thin walls, I can hear him on the phone—in his little-boy voice, talking erotic baby gibberish—to Ann or Priscilla. It would go on for hours. I'd relocate myself across the room, far away from the schizoid scene.

There's a light tapping on the trailer door.

"Who? Wha'?" calls the King.

"Ready to go, boss." It's Richard's silky drawl.

It's time. I unfurl myself from the chair, grateful for the interruption. His oscillating thing between Ann and Priscilla is getting to my prune. Thing is, neither one stirs my finely honed libido. Priscilla is like a hunk of cardboard—Ann is bogus. If I had to choose between them, it would be Ann. Maybe...Why the hell am I dwelling on Elvis' problem? He's not about to hook up with Ann. Down deep, it's Priscilla. He loves her. He knows it. I know it...

I leave the coolness of the trailer and get to work on my own puny dilemmas. This whip-snapping fast life is exhausting. Dealing with the daily drill of moviemaking and its myriad personalities, and Elvis, along with his ever-present minion. I'm beat. A week old banana peel has nothing on me.

Hallelujah! Tomorrow we leave Las Vegas, back to Los Angeles—leaving the hypnotic cacophony of the casinos, the acrid cigarette smoke, clacking chips, endlessly-whining slot machines. Adios, Sin City.

❧

I'm in L.A. with Marilyn Brown. This Miss has a bit of pluck, does her own thing, super sex, supreme sense of humor—but she's promiscuous. "But she's promiscuous," like I'm a saint. It's nineteen sixty-three. Monumental changes going down in our country. Folks checking out all kinds of bullshit—busting free, fuck the system, the war, the bra, the draft card, the tie, apple pie...I'm ranting.

I'm kicked back, staring at the tube. A news commentator is carrying on about the usual stuff, the Arabs and the Israelis. Black hair—nice looking guy—familiar face—Stan Bohrman! We joined the Air Force together. Went through basic training together. We were neighbors—kids together. The man is doing alright. Damn. Good for him...Shit, what the hell am I doing with my life?

I'm in the shadows of the theater, at Santa Monica College, I'm appraising the scene. The movie crew is preparing the stage for a dance sequence for "Viva Las Vegas" where Elvis and Ann Margaret dance together. I'm watching the whole procedure go down. First, the choreographer teaches Lance Lagault the routine, then Lance teaches the routine to Elvis. I'm duly impressed. Elvis learns the moves in a matter of minutes. Bam! Let's roll. The King is ready to kick up his famous heels. No laborious rehearsal, a few times through with Ann, then it's action. The song is "Come on Everybody." They are totally connected—getting down to some delightful hoofing.

❧

It's a sunny day. I'm cruising-cool on Sunset Blvd in my spit-polish, candy-apple Austin Healy. White tonneau cover, shiny chrome wheels—hey, this is Hollywood, I'm right there with everyone else, pretending like I know what the hell I'm doing. From the car behind me, someone is calling my name. "Salvatore, Salvatore." I do a half twist. It's Sharon Tate.

"Ey hi, Sharon."

"I'll treat you to lunch."

"Cool."

"Follow me."

I do, to Martoni's Italian Restaurant on Cahuenga Boulevard. For the next two hours, we dine, we wine, talk, laugh, sing. This is a real person. Absolutely no trace of superior bullshit. She's wonderful. I'm privileged to know her.

∞

Back to Graceland. I'm on standby, waiting for Elvis to summon me into his chilly chambers (tinfoil covers all the windows blocking out every sliver of sunlight). He's been holed up in his cold dark cave for over a week. What have I been doing?

A digression...I've been shtupping an authentic Southern Belle. One of Elvis' former girlfriends. Elvis arranged our meeting. She's a beauty, in her late twenties, independent, pleasant, she's—what can I say? She's nice. What the hell. She's clean, and I'm in no mood to sniff around for fresh pussy. So, it's like, I grab a few jazz albums, hit the best Mexican restaurant in town (mediocre compared to Los Angeles), sip a few hefty margaritas, split to her modest apartment on the outskirts of town, smoke a joint, pop an album onto the turntable, sip of wine, then—hit it. The sex is like, well, let me put it this way, you would have to stand up on your tiptoes to barely reach mediocre. Still, it's something to do, and breaking away from the parameters of the King's world keeps me cool.

So a few nights ago it's post-coital time, I'm leisurely dressing in my lady's bathroom after a flawlessly crummy roll-in-the-hay. She fucks like a senior citizen Quaker. I hear the intrusive "ding a ping a ding," the sound of her chiming doorbell. Someone is pressing hard. "Oh Christ! Shit! I think it's him," she blurts.

"Say wha', who?"

"My ex-boyfriend," she snaps, slithering into her tight red dress.

"Ya who, wha, boyfriend?"

"Just a sec," she mellifluously calls out to the untimely visitor.

"Your boyfriend?"

"Ex."

"Does he know that?"

"Kinda."

I'm into a cold sweat. A few nights ago, Elvis and Allen were teasing me about her about-to-be-released-from-prison jealous boyfriend. His name is Billy Joe, Timmy Tom, or Jimmy Bob, Henry Joe? Jesus, the South is something else with names. She takes a deep breath and bravely answers the door. With unfettered haste, I zip up my trousers, button my shirt and straighten my hair.

"Oh, it's Billy Dicky," I hear her feigned delightful cry coming from the living room. That's it, Billy Dicky! Is that the name Elvis said? Billy Dicky? Fucking Billy Dicky. Out of prison. He's here. Damn. I really don't need this. I wipe beads of sweat from my brow and cautiously slip into the living room. He looks mean, weasel-eyed, built like a tractor. The moment calls for seamless strategy.

"Sal, this is Billy Dicky," she anxiously squeaks.

"Hi, Billy Dicky," I reply in my finest falsetto voice, hoping he'll think that I'm a little light in the loafers. Before he has a chance to respond, I say, "Oh, just a minute, I've got to show you something, I'll be right back."

I split. For the next twenty minutes I'm trotting along as if I knew where I was going. I'm lost, in a black neighborhood. Not a cab in sight. If this were Watts in Los Angeles, I'd be more than a little apprehensive. No bad vibe here. It's a steamy-hot summer night. Slowing down to a walk, I get a whiff of jasmine and barbecue sauce, hear folks singing gospel music...This is the South and these people are for real.

I'm having a primo gestalt...I spot a cab, wave, wave, the cab stops, I get in—where to? Beale Street. Half an hour later, I'm in a Beale Street joint, digging a steaming band working the blues. The real stuff. Save leaving my Miles Davis albums at the lady's place, it's been a neat night.

❧

I'm hanging around waiting to do Elvis' hair. Meanwhile I'm focusing—getting into an absolutely necessary mindset. With the King, you never know what kind of mood he's in. Is it the Rudy Valentino bag? Where I do his hair flat to his head, then, donned in shiny black silky duds, sash the whole shot—says he's part Italian. For hours he exhorts the smooth "Rudolph Valentino style" and his manhood. Or conversely, the "karate thing." Talking about Yamamoto, a tough-ass master of karate who kills bulls with one punch to their hearts. Or, Hank Slamansky, another kick-ass master—who's mastered the art of dislocation. You throw a punch at this guy and your arms and shoulders will be on backwards. Or, is he "The Singer"—that's a good one, I can get into that. We listen to music, blues, Ink Spots, gospel—he gets "down" on gospel. When he sings gospel, he "knows" what he's singing about. I'm not saying times are all bad—no, half the time it's great, wonderful to be with him.

Unfortunately, other times he's totally fucked up. His mouth and eyes wide, strands of hair stuck to his damp forehead, twitchy movements, his thinking confused. Then he's a child. Thoughts of childhood dwell in his mind, and if I were to ask him something sensibly, he would likely answer in an innocent reverential voice. Will he swing to the man? Or have more confidence as a boy? Does the boy misunderstand the man? I know, it's heavy shit, his gigantic anxieties wear me out. What's he into today? What the hell does he do locked up in his room for days at a time? The whole world is at his beck and call, yet there he is, in his room, snug, like a snail in its shell. The King of Graceland.

As for the Queen of Graceland, Priscilla, during the day she's usually busy visiting the beauty salon or maybe gallivanting around town with a couple of girlfriends. I really don't know what and I really don't care. Meanwhile, Elvis is whacked out, stoned on uppers and downers, drifting and dreaming, fleeing from the real world, creating his own universe, far from the Hollywood Star bullshit, floating in a strange perverse way until he settles into another part of himself, leaving his narcissism, his greatness, the shaky-legged icon, the hound dog, the blue suede shoes, as he dives into a metaphysical universe, the place with no name, the "other side." He's special and he knows it. Surely his specialness will buy him a ticket to the unknown, maybe creak open a cosmic door or two.

How about me? What the hell am I doing? Secluded from the Guys and rapping all kinds of Zen stuff to Elvis like I know what I'm talking about. Most times, Elvis sits still, bows his head and listens attentively to what I'm sputtering on about. Still, most of the time I feel like I'm talking too much and too glibly, yet I roll along laying out a viewpoint or two about existence. Hey, I'm into that stuff too. Whatever we rap about, invariably within the next day or two, when I'm supposed to be out of sight, I hear Elvis spouting almost verbatim stuff that I've said in our rapping sessions as if it were his own words.

What's the Graceland Gestalt? Occasionally, after the midnight movies, there's a party for a few friends and moochers. It's always the same, the ladies' lusty eyes glued to Elvis, the envious guys fawning all over him, forever polishing the Apple. I do a run through, then quickly descend to my solitary quarters downstairs and contemplate reality. It's, how would Jay put it, kicky. Positively kicky. Elvis is an institution. Of course that has an effect on me. Through him, I see things in a another way. Things I would not ordinarily see and hear. Like the reactions people have when they meet him, their genuine insincerity an embarrassment to witness. Here's a guy, the personification of hot sex all over the world. Incredible. How the hell does anyone live up to that image? It's got to drain your brain trying to lead a normal life with that kind of bullshit going down. The contradiction is massive. On the one hand, he gets fucked up trying to get away from the bullshit, on the other, he feeds on the adulation, the swoons and ecstatic moans of the public and gets high from that. The fact remains that he's a great artist, and I get to be up close and see what a great artist is all about.

Okay, he's ready for me. I'm tapping on the King's dank door. Charlie opens the door. Peeping over his shoulder, I see Elvis—skipper's hat askew, bloated—man, he's gained about twenty pounds. I'm startled. I shouldn't be. Elvis has the table manners of a monitor lizard. With his hands, he rips, tears and smothers his prey with tons of salt and pepper, then jams it all into his mouth. Gross.

Elvis motions for Charlie to split. That's a sure sign that he wants to talk. Elvis rarely raps about the big themes—God, destiny, cosmic savvy—around the Guys. With me it's full throttle. Sometimes I'm into it, other times it's draining. But he can be funny, like the time he jumped onto a table and spontaneously delivered a fiery evangelical message street-style. "Ol' Jesus knew he was fucked. Dragging that big ol' cross through town. Fucked up folks throwing rocks at his skinny celestial ass. The man is freaking. He's a carpenter, he knows about nails and wood and shit. He knows they're gonna hammer his ass to that big ol' chunk of oak."

He's holding a book, which he carefully places onto the barber chair. He removes his skipper's cap. His hair is damp and matted tight to his head. Warily, he circles the barber chair as if it were booby trapped.

"Want to wash my hair first?" he asks in a cool *sotto voce* voice.

"Yes. Definitely. Yes," I do the *sotto voce* thing too.

He sits down at the bathroom sink—I hand him a folded hand towel, he covers his eyes with the towel and lowers his head into the sink basin. I get to work sudsing his funky hair. I catch a glimpse of the book he's placed on the barber chair.

"Edger Cayce. Is that what you're reading?" I ask.

"Uh huh, he's got something going on," mumbles the King.

"He's into a Blavatsky trip."

"Bla-who?"

"Blavatsky. Madam Blavatsky. Communicating with the spirits. Stuff like that."

"I'll get the book."

"Don't bother, man. Cayce, Blavatsky. It's all slathered in bullshit. But I read them anyhow, to recognize baloney when it comes my way."

Elvis raises his head slowly from the sink basin. He's taciturn. I wrap a towel around his head. He picks up the Cayce book from the barber chair and tosses it aside. He eyes the chair a few seconds before he commits to sitting in it. He eases into the chair while staring straight and hard at his mirrored image. "Slathered?"

"To spread thickly."

Elvis looks at his reflected self. "My face," he says flatly.

"Zen asks, 'What was your original face before your mother and father were born?' Trippy, huh?"

"What's it mean?"

"That's the trip. You have to work out that answer yourself."

Elvis sighs and sinks deeper into the chair. I get busy with the hair thing.

"What else?"

"What else? Let's see, ah, wait a minute, it's coming. Okay, dig this. You cannot describe it or draw it. You cannot praise it enough or perceive it. No place can be found in which to put the original face. It will not disappear, even when the universe is destroyed."

"Is that Zen stuff?"

"Yeah, Mumon, Zen monk."

Another long sigh from Elvis. It's tacitly understood that it's time for me to shut up. Is he pissed? I never know if I've said the wrong or right thing. I'm really not into this touchy shit. It's unnatural for me to edit my thinking in conversation lest I get into a taboo area. He's innocent, gullible and vulnerable. He keeps asking me about the cosmos and shit. Half the time I don't know what the hell I'm saying. From now on I just give my name, rank and serial number. He's got to find his own way through "The world of ten thousand things."

After a few silent minutes, Elvis presses a nearby speaker button. "Get Charlie," he says into the speaker.

Sonny's voice quickly responds. "Right away, boss." In a minute, Charlie is standing behind me.

"Did you get them yet?" Elvis asks Charlie.

"They're there right now."

"How about the one with the black guy?"

"Sydney Poitier."

"At midnight?"

"Whenever your ready, Elvis."

There's a pause. Elvis doesn't look too happy. Charlie picks up on his vibe and steps into his court jester routine. I gotta say, when Charlie gets cooking on the "down home" country jive, it's always funny stuff and it usually garners a few laughs from Elvis.

Two hours hence—hair cut, hair dyed, hair set, ready for the cinema. He goes through all this trouble to sit in a dinky theater with the Guys and a couple dozen faithful fans, viewing movies at three o'clock in the morning. He never lets his public down. He's Elvis Presley...

∽♪∽

Back to West Hollywood, my home turf. While I was away, Camy has moved out of her apartment. She must have spotted me. Marilyn has her own apartment, but most of the time she stays at my place. The more we are together, the more I like it. Love it?...Elvis and the Guys won't be here for two more weeks. It's a welcome moratorium from the King and his Guys. Gives me time to explore my own world—and explore I righteously do. On weekends, Marilyn and I drop LSD. I enter the Zen zone. Finding the mind. Probing the mind. Losing the mind. "Is-ness" of being. Ego, Super Ego, the super-duper Ego, Haiku, Koans. Hey, I'm rolling. It's the sixties, and I'm damn happy to be alive.

Two weeks later. Another film, out in the country in Hidden Valley, fifty miles west of Los Angeles. We're on location for a movie called "Roustabout." Halcyon country roads, lined with vintage oak trees, bright chalk-white fences, corrals, the imposing presence of thoroughbred horses peacefully romping. It's a beautiful property surrounding a rather modest ranch house, which was formerly owned by the late actor Alan Ladd. Even with all the beautiful scenery, the welcome smell of fresh air and summer roses, chirping crickets and singing birds, it's the pits.

The director John Rich doesn't appreciate Elvis' Guys hanging around the set. I do Elvis' hair in his trailer dressing room, double-time, in between takes. The vibe on the set is morose compared to the snap-crackle-pop of Las Vegas. The Guys' silly-ass pranks have become wearily predictable, and mordant wit is nowhere to be found. The pits—except for one grand lady, the exceptional Barbara Stanwyck. A first-class person. A real person. Doesn't lay that "Hollywood speak" on you. She's personable. In between takes, she hangs with the crew and joins in on their friendly banter. I've had a couple of conversations with her, I felt like her younger brother. Nothing bogus about this lady.

I've discovered a cozy spot on the grass under an inveterate oak tree within earshot of the film shooting. This is where I spend most of the day. Kicked back, summarizing mundane realities. It's not a bad gig. Bread's good. High-line living. But it's like it's the King's planet and I'm just a guest on it. The Elvis Presley thing—a blazing icon. It's a full time job being "Elvis Presley." High voltage stuff—too intense for me.

Here's the program. A day shooting out in Hidden Valley, then a fifty-mile freeway battle back to my apartment in West Hollywood. I've been doing some heavy thinking while snaking my way along the busy freeway. Do I stay with the King? Keep the gig? Has it come to an end? My moves are dictated by his needs. That kinda fucks up the spontaneity in my personal life. Maybe the good times are worth the whole trip? Maybe...I don't know. I'm just tripping...

Two months later, the making of "Roustabout" is done. Fini. The whole thing was a downer. I don't want to talk about it. It's depressing. I'm hanging in my apartment, waiting for the Kings' call for me to do his hair. It's been four full days of impeccable vacillation. Come to the house at four o'clock. Right. I prepare, I anticipate, I'm ready to go. Another call—make that five o'clock tomorrow. Right. Another call. Make that three o'clock the day after tomorrow. Right, etc. Okay, Elvis has changed his mind. Okay, I'm getting paid for sitting around. That's my rationale. The fifth day I get a call from Alan Fortis—come up and do Elvis' hair as soon as possible.

Hallelujah! Snippity-snap, I get my act together, rapido, slide into my candy-apple Austin Healy wheels and zoom to Elvis' Bel Air digs. I maneuver through the usual pimply fans camping at the King's front gate and inform the speaker box that I'm here.

Finally, I'm pressing on the King's chiming doorbell. In two blinks, Li'l Billy answers the door. Whoa—I don't see Li'l Billy's usual elfin grin—he's tight-eyed and intense—his dander is definitely way up. The air is humming with anxiety. "'Bout time y'all showed up," says Li'l Billy in a clipped voice.

I'm not ready for Li'l Billy's wrath. What the hell is he talking about? I've been waiting for days. I take a deep breath and let it pass. "Is Joe around?" I pointedly ask. Joe and Sonny are the only two guys I can talk to and get a straight answer.

"Not here tonight," snaps Li'l Billy as he hastily ushers me into an adjacent room. I sit and wait for Elvis. The room is big and round with a domed twenty-foot high ceiling. There's a few scattered ersatz sofas and armchairs, and a kelly-green pool table presiding in the center of the room like a huge water lily. While I'm waiting, I sit and stare at the water lily—getting into its greenness, like a frog...Now I'm still. Centered. Passive. That's what one does when one is a little frog in a big pond. I hear anxious whispers coming from the shadowy hallway—

blows my frog trip. Sounds like Li'l Billy, Charlie and Richard Davis. What's the dispute? Impossible to say. Elvis has a impressive array of kaleidoscopic moods. Could be anything. I'm antsy. Sitting. Pondering. Antsy...

Either the pool table or I have to make a move. Enough already...
"Hey, Billy Boy," I call out.

I hear the staccato report of boot heels striking the hardwood floor. Uneven. Uncertain. Little Billy is standing over me.

"What is it?" he croaks, his face all scrunchy like a constipated ferret.

"I'm leaving. If Elvis wants me, tell him I'll see him tomorrow."

Li'l Billy looks hard and squinty—his face turns the color of pink Chablis.

"Y'all better stick around heah, boy, if you want to keep your job," he says threateningly.

That's all I need.

"Tell Elvis, if that's the way he feels, he can have the job."

"Y'all saying that y'all quitting?" says Li'l Billy, hawking his throat and shaking his head in disbelief.

"I'll call tomorrow," I candidly respond.

His eyes go cold. "Y'all gone crazy?"

I split.

I'm up half the night thinking about whether I should quit the gig or stay on. Strip Elvis of the outrageous bullshit that stamps him as a worldwide icon and you find a tender and loving, honest-to-God, blue-ribbon human being. That's the Elvis I know. That's the one I respect. I toss and turn, trying to figure out who will take my place with him. Someone with more than a modicum of humility. Someone who can rap about the metaphysical, philosophical and religious realms. At dawn I finally have it. Larry Geller. Larry is a hairdresser at Jay's shop. He's soft-spoken, mannerly—I'm sure Elvis will be pleased with him.

I call Larry, tell him what's going on—ask him if he would like the gig with Elvis. "Are you kidding?" he asks. I assure him that I'm not kidding. He's delighted and appreciative that I would recommend him for the gig. I assure Larry that he's the right guy for Elvis. I call Elvis. Talk to Allen Fortis. I tell Allen that I'm quitting the gig. Stone silence, followed by a low groan. I further tell Allen that I found someone to replace me. Another low groan. (Later on, I learned what the groaning was all about. Elvis had fired him and a couple of the Guys because they didn't talk to me properly. But, as usual, Elvis rehired them a couple of weeks later).

Later on in the day, Larry comes over to my apartment for a briefing session about Elvis and his ways. I'm helping him ease into the day-to-day dynamics of the Elvis Presley cosmology. I tell him, be prepared to spend endless hours in the bathroom with Elvis talking about all kinds of celestial, ethereal and transcendental stuff. I tell him how Elvis was most impressed when, one time after having cut his hair, I swept the floor clean of his hair and Elvis says, "You didn't have to do that." And I say, "I made the mess, I'll clean it up." Like I said, Elvis was impressed.

Larry is hanging onto every word I say. He keeps repeating, "No kidding, tell me more." I go on. Be alert and ready for the subtle parameters of familiarity, know when to dummy up, etc. After a couple of hours, I wish Larry good luck and tell him to never forget that when you peel off the Hollywood bullshit, he'll find that Mr. Elvis Presley is one of the finest human beings he will ever know. Larry thanked me profusely for my time and my concern that he do well with the King.

Whew! It's over. It was, how shall I say, "interesting." Any regrets? No, it was the right thing to do. I had to see for myself what Hollywood is all about. I've learned more than I want to know. All my previous curiosities have long since vanished. I can't deny the excitement, the grandeur. It's a delusive reality which, for awhile, I carried over into my own world. I wanted to see how far I would get beyond myself. Hollywood celebs—and I've been exposed to many—are adulation junkies, who've got to have public esteem, finding comfort in flatteries and the narcissistic fix. It stokes the id, you transcend the ordinary business of daily life, you walk around farting through silk. That's Hollywood fame and it's all nonsense.

Here I am, standing beside the quintessential emblem of Hollywood fame. I don't see Elvis that way. I don't know why. To me, Elvis is a guy, a hell of a guy, and a hell of a talent. I can see his heavy addiction coming on slowly, like a locomotive chugging uphill. He's gonna fall, he's starting to topple already. Hey, what can I do? I'm not about to meddle in his life. The Guys don't say shit about his condition, they have been around him a lot longer than me. Maybe Elvis can handle it. Shit, I don't know. If the guy wasn't "Elvis," I could hang with the man. We could be friends, maybe good friends. However it's not written in the stars, and I'm back to my own realities. I'm full up to my Adam's Apple with Tinsel Town effluvia. It's time for me to slip back into my groove. Get some spontaneity going in my life. Karate lessons with Jay, playing jazz with fellow musicians, getting mellow with Marilyn. It doesn't sound like much compared to the fast-lane, high-end living, but I'm unshackled, and that keeps me sane.

CHAPTER EIGHT

I'm winding up Benedict Canyon, heading for Jay's house. I haven't seen him in a week, at which time he gave me a surprise 31st birthday party at his house. About forty or fifty people were buzzing around the pool—artists, hairstylists, a few actors and a few of my friends. Everyone was into raising their consciousness via LSD, mescaline, mushrooms, grass, yoga and a variety of mind-probing methods, from Freud to Reichian, Alpert to Leary.

Al Lapin was there, fervently gesticulating, and as always delivering a loud and compelling existential sermon. "Deah, people. Deah, deah, people. You're all a bunch of assholes! Drop all the bullshit games. Rid yourself of the mind-cluttering crap! Clear yourself! Do you see me?! Do you see?" When Al saw me, he waved and shouted, "There is no birthday! Happy birthless day!" followed by an ironic laugh and "Happy birthless day, asshole!" I love this man.

I slip into my allotted parking slot, check out my wristwatch (Elvis' Christmas gift to me). I gave him a medal, its inscription reads, "We shall overcome." He wore it a few times. At least he didn't throw it away. It's getting late. Jay is always, always late for everything. I'm the opposite. I'm telling myself, "Relax, go with the flow," but it's not working. I can sense Jay's high energy from out here in the parking lot. It's gonna be trippy—it's always trippy with the Jason.

I'm in Jay's bedroom. Jay is in the dressing room (the same dressing room in which Paul Bern, Jean Harlow's husband, committed suicide). He's preparing for tonight's occasion—the International Karate Meet, which our venerable karate instructor Ed Parker has diligently organized and produced, and at which Jay will be the presenter of a winner's trophy.

"We don't have much time," I call out.

"There's some smoke on the nightstand, roll a few will ya?" is Jay's muffled reply from upstairs.

"Let's get our asses going, man."

"Don't get all twitchy now."

Ten minutes flash by. I'm putting the finishing touches on rolling the third joint. Jay, looking natty as ever, leaps into the room. "How do I look?" he says, slapping his black-leather driving gloves across the elephant-hair bracelet on his wrist.

"Transparent," I say as I hand Jay the joints.

"Let's go, man."

"My boy, we are on our fucking way. First a couple of puffs." As we split the doobie, Jay gives me a squint and a grin. "I have a surprise," he announces.

"Please man, you and your surprises. The last surprise, the Elvis thing, wore me out, I can't take another surprise like that, man."

"Dig it...You know that guy Ed has been telling us about?"

"Bruce Lee?"

"Yeah, Bruce Lee!"

Ed Parker has been telling us about this fantastic, twenty-four year old guy, a martial arts master, unknown, except in the martial arts circles. "So?" I say.

"So, he's gonna be there tonight at the meet," says Jay smoothing out his hair with his fingers.

"Great...To compete?"

"No. But Ed says he's gonna do a demo."

"Let's go, Jason. I'm into it."

"Yeah, we gotta drive." A couple more hits, and we're out the door.

In a minute, we're chug-a-lugging down Benedict Canyon onto Sunset Boulevard, then onto the 405 freeway. Jay lead-foots the gas pedal, whooshing the Cobra to a speed of ninety-five miles an hour in about three seconds. Now we're weaving in, out and around the traffic like we owned the freeway. It's un-fucking canny. Not a cop in sight. I go three miles over the speed limit, I have two squad cars on my ass. Pronto. That's the way it goes. Jay drives like a nut, but nothing ever happens to him. Un-fucking canny.

We arrive at the arena in world-record time. At least five thousand spectators, plus contestants from all parts of the world, are in devoted attendance. Jay, being a presenter of a trophy, scoots off to the "celebrity seating area" in the first row. I'm twenty rows behind, sandwiched between two humongous sumo wrestlers. It's fascinating to watch the martial arts contestants go through their paces. The years of discipline and training it must have taken to achieve such skill.

However, after watching twenty or thirty contestants and watching Jay gleefully present the winner with a shiny trophy, my interest is rapidly abating. Like Tillie the barber says, "You see one log, you've seen them all."

When Bruce Lee comes out, an expectant hush hangs over the arena. Is it a hype? Is he for real? Bruce does the ritual humble bowing bit, then bam! He springs at least six feet straight up, throws about eight hundred punches before he hits the ground, then rolls around the floor like a basketball, then spreads out flat like a crab, then jumps and twists like a panther, then, shit—man, he just went on and on—every move impeccable. The guy has some major chops, no doubt about that. Big time moves...I'm profoundly impressed.

On our speedy return freeway flight, Jay is running on about how we have to study with Bruce Lee. "We gotta do it, man. We gotta study with the guy," says Jay.

"I'm with that, man."

"We gotta do it. You saw that stuff, man. Jesus, he was a fucking blur, a fucking blur."

"Unreal. That's what it is."

"He's a little cat too."

"Yeah, he is. In this case, size isn't everything, man."

"Salvatore, my man, we're gonna study with him."

"Neat."

"I'll get on it."

"Neat."

"Yeah...I'll get on it."

And get on it he did. Two weeks later, Bruce Lee comes to Jay's house to give us private instruction in his method of the martial arts. After a quick cup of green tea, we go to the "fighting room" which Jay has recently converted from a bedroom.

The first thing Bruce tells me is to stand in front of him and to throw a punch at his chest as fast as I can. For real, no pulling punches. I'm jittery—I know he's going to lay some serious moves on me. I look blankly at Jay in the corner of the room. He's grinning, fingers the "okay" sign. Shit, what's this little guy have in mind for me? Avanti. I plant my feet firmly on the floor, bend my legs slightly and get into a solid position. I take a deep breath and let fly one of the better punches of all time, straight as a Comanche arrow, with all the power my lungs can muster. Zam! He's gone! Nowhere in sight. Nada, niente. It's like a magic act or something. I have this big perplexed "huh" look on my face, I can feel it. Where the hell is he? I look at Jay, he's cracking up. I turn my head around and there's Bruce in a knee-high crouch behind my right ankle, his fingers shaped like a tiger's claw two inches away from the family jewels. Jay is laughing his ass off while jabbing his fingers at Bruce, then back to me.

Bruce comes over to Jay's house once a week. A couple cups of hot green tea, then we get into it. Bruce is showing us all kinds of stuff. How to power punch using your lats, long punch, short punch, finger-length punch—how to move and bend and breath—to "strike at emptiness" (Bruce's favorite phrase) which he repeats throughout our lessons. Another one is "the usefulness of a bowl is in its emptiness."

Bruce and I absolutely "connect" in the Zen Zone. There's a game we play, straight out of the "Pink Panther" where Inspector Clouseau's valet hides somewhere in the house ready to attack. Inspector Clouseau, not knowing where the attack will come from, creeps and slithers through the house, ready to defeat the sneaky attacker. Bruce, playing the role of the valet, takes it a step further. He doesn't hide and he lets you know up front that he will strike within ten minutes. Now we try and maintain a state of "prepared unpreparedness." It could happen any second, or nine minutes from now, or at the end of our lesson. We could be talking about a movie, a book, scratching our ass, whatever, trying to relax and flow with the "now" while at the same time being alert and ready to defend ourselves. Of course, Bruce always nails both our asses the instant our minds stray. That's the kind of stuff I'm into. I don't give a damn about breaking boards or smashing someone's breastbones.

After a couple of months of training with Bruce, I'm in optimum shape. My senses are popping. One morning, the game carries over into breakfast. Jay, Bruce and I are pleasantly chatting at the breakfast table. My napkin falls off the table—intuitively, without bifurcation, I grab it in midair. At that very instant my other hand blocks Bruce's hand-chopping strike meant for the side of my head. Whoa...To this day, I don't know how it happened. Bruce gives me a big approving smile, then we chant in unison, "The usefulness of a bowl is in its emptiness." That day I learned something. Alright, maybe all that esoteric knowledge and two bucks might get me a bean burrito, but for me it was a sterling epiphany.

A few nights later, Bruce, Jay and I fall by the Whiskey A-Go-Go nightclub on Sunset. The place is overflowing with "Hollywood" gentry. Over the cacophonous din, Johnny Rivers is singing "Memphis, Tennessee." We meld into the crowd and settle in a corner of the room, unscathed, unnoticed.

Jay gets busy eyeballing the ladies on the sardine-packed dance floor. His eyes narrow when he spots a lantern-jawed, barrel-chested monster descending the crowded stairwell. From the look on Jay's contorted face, the guy is the enemy. "Watch this," says Jay with a subtle nod of his head.

"Wha'cha got, man?"

"This guy is a real asshole."

"An asshole with big bumpy muscles, I might bring to your attention, Jason."

"Fuck 'em," says Jay.

Jay takes a deep breath, then saunters over to the guy—who towers over Jay like a giraffe—and commences to guilelessly provoke him. I can't hear what Jay is saying, what with Mr. Rivers carrying on about Memphis and all, but using my lip-reading skills I can see that he's vehemently disgorging a slew of nasties onto the dude. I can also see that the monster is righteously pissed off. I sense that Jay has something up the ol' perennial sleeve. Bruce and I are watching the whole scene go down. After a couple of minutes of frisky diatribe, Jay rejoins us. He's all puffy. "Fuckin' jerk," splutters Jay.

"Big jerk. Big muscles," I realistically add.

Over Jay's shoulder I see the monster coming our way, slit-eyed and egregiously bellicose. He has a few hardcore expletives of his own and tells Jay if he wasn't such a little shit he would break his back, etc. Jay, practically spitting in his face, tells the guy to go fuck himself. As Jay and the monster continue trading threats, it's blatantly obvious that they're definitely heading for a combative situation. I catch Bruce's stoic eye. He's composed. Finally the monster has had enough. He tightens his gun-boat fists threateningly, figuring Jay will back off. Jay, defiant as a cornered mongoose, ratchets up his obscenities.

Now I'm peering at Bruce. He remains cool and impassive. The monster catapults a powerhouse punch. Varoom! Bruce goes into action. Like a hungry tiger pouncing on a T-bone steak, shoving Jay aside, Bruce simultaneously defects the monster's mega-punch while expertly sinking two consummate blows deep into the guy's solar plexus. The guy drops to the floor gasping for air. Bruce drags him to a nearby wall, props him upright, tells him to take deep breaths and that he'll be alright in a few minutes. A few folks at the bar watch the whole scene happen. I hear "Who the hell is that Chinaman?" and "Did you catch that action?" We split.

Once outside the Whiskey, Bruce is fuming. He tells Jay straight and level, "Don't ever pull that shit again." Bruce knew he was being used. Jay bows Hindu-style to Bruce and swears he will never do it again.

Later on, leaning over breakfast at Ollie Hammond's, I ask Jay what it was all about with the Bruce thing. "I just had to see him do something for real, man," says Jay cracking with laughter. "Did you catch those punches, man? A fuckin' blur. Man, that big asshole dropped like a bowling ball." Now Jay cracks up laughing. As usual, so do I.

CHAPTER NINE

Marilyn and I are joined in holy matrimony by the local spiritualist/psychic/ minister Genie Allen. She's a grandmotherly woman with keen twinkling eyes that nail you like a prison searchlight. She says I'm an old soul and have a guardian on each of my shoulders and that Marilyn and I will be soul mates forever. Hey, I'm listening, it's better than hearing that I'm an asshole and our marriage doesn't have a chance in hell, although that's what I'm thinking. It's kinda dumb getting married at a time like this. This is nineteen sixty-five, the zeitgeist is free love, free sex, free spirit, unshackle your ass from the bullshit social mores. So why am I getting married? I'm insecure and I don't want to lose her? It's an ego thing? I love her? Hell, I don't know...We lease a cozy cottage in Laurel Canyon, a mecca for musicians. Rock and blues music bursts out of the canyon like a breaching whale.

Life's vicissitudes again. Today I'm sad. Al Lapin, the grizzly Guru of Dianetics, died today. Committed suicide. He lost his shampoo business. Allegedly, he was swindled out of his partnership by his brothers. That's cold—pushed Al over the top. He freaked. Last time I had seen him, he was raving mad. Plopping his hands onto my shoulders, clamping hard like a vice, then looking deep into my eyes, then past the eyes to the Ego, the Superego, the Id, the Ictus—right down to the mental "blow of breath" from the Buddha. The great "unknown." For a good two minutes he's staring straight into me. Then, slowly and pathetically, he whispers, "I'm lost. Lost." Desperate tears rolled down his sullen and deeply creviced cheeks. Jesus, I don't know what to say. I mean, what the hell do I say? Here's a guy who rode high above the common quarrelsome fray, a guy with cosmic consciousness savvy, an enlightened man, crumbling to dust before my eyes. Oddly, at that very moment, all I could think about was we don't know shit. Nothing. We think we know, but we don't know shit. The mind that does not know "is" the Buddha. I'm gonna hang with that thought, it helps me get out of bed in the morning.

My cash, is rapidly dwindling, I'm thinking about going back to work at Jay's shop. I check it out. It's not the same. The once palpitating aura is gone and my fascination with movie stars has long since evaporated. It's different now. Jay's shop has changed, as all things do. Oh, business is booming and the shop is methodically in order, but that "special" spark is gone. The clientele is textbook common. The type that look at each other for a viewpoint, what interests one interests all. That kind of commonality. Not cool. The rich variety of personalities, the talk, the rhythm—gone. That's the way it is, it's here and then it's not here.

Under the influence of these surroundings, I'm acting as if I'd thought it all out. Not really, but I do know I've got to be unimpeded, away from human beings imitating other human beings, where one question sounds like another. I have no ambition to be in the right against the majority, however my own inquiries are in another direction. I have a high regard for the ordinary happiness of everyday living. I've seen up close what public esteem can do to a person, never again to enjoy being unnoticed. Fuck that. Anyhow, Jay's shop is not for me. What's next? Andiamo.

Jay is jamming, doing his thing, becoming a men's hairdressing star. He's in magazines, on television, radio. At the moment, he's in New York City appearing on the TV shows. I've decided to go with my friend Rick, who has a shop on La Cienega next door to the Bantam Cock restaurant. Rick glides around in a hyper bubble, vigorously preoccupied, chomping on Chiclets and dragging on Kool filtered cigarettes.

Charlton Heston comes in for a haircut, Rick asks him his name, Charlton tells him. Rick asks, "How do you spell that"? Charlton patiently spells out his name. Rick looks up at him and says, "Oh yeah, Moses, right, Moses." Charlton took it well, no uppity attitude—he became a frequent client of the shop.

Lenny Bruce is also one of Rick's clients. Lenny is a private guy, with Jewish grief written across his forehead, not a hint of humor. Rick is doing a house call at Lenny's place in the hills above Sunset. Big house—bereft of furniture, save one flimsy card table and a floor lamp with its shade askew.

Lenny's mother lives in the house. Lenny camps in a cottage on the back property. The cottage is a monument to squalor, with mounds of legal books and documents, newspapers scattered on the floor, a dusty vintage typewriter, a foul odor emitting from the toilet—the room says "junkie." Lenny scoops up a handful of legal papers while dragging a flimsy wooden chair across the room. He places a chair precisely under a lonely light bulb. He mumbles something about his haircut to Rick—Rick mumbles back. Now Lenny flops onto the creaky chair, takes a deep breath, exhales and sighs, then burrows into the legal papers. I sink to the funky floor into a not-so-cozy squat.

Silence—except for pages fervently flipping. Forty minutes slip by, then it's over. Rick, in slow motion, gingerly removes the haircloth from Lenny's hunched shoulders. Rick is packing his gear. Finally Lenny straightens up, pans the room, looks at Rick, then me. He forces an anemic smile. I give him a phony smile back. A few more mumbles between him and Rick, then we split.

Winding down the hill, I ask Rick what that was all about. Is he always so dreary? Rick says no, sometimes they talk about all kinds of stuff—and that Lenny has a laser-beam weapon-thing taken from an Army tank, and that the beam is pinpointed on Schwabs drugstore on Sunset Boulevard. Anyway, that's the Lenny Bruce trip.

A few months clippity-snip by, I'm slowly rebuilding a clientele. It's lunchtime—Bruce Lee drops by the shop—we rendezvous with Jay at Ollie Hammond's. Jay tells me that he's hooking-up Bruce with Bill Dozier (one of Jay's big producer clients) for the role of Kato in the "Green Hornet" television series. Getting the role would be a quantum leap for Bruce's inchoate career. Bruce tells us he won't be able to teach us on a regular basis, having to direct his time and energy on showbiz. I thank him for the honor of his martial arts teaching.

I tell Jay that I'm opening my own shop. He's delighted, says I'll do well. Jay reassures me that he still plans to expand his business, start a line of cosmetics for men, followed by a charm school for men. When that happens, he reiterates, I'm to be his personal advisor. It sounds good, but right now I have to get kicking with my own karma.

After a year, it's time for me to leave Rick's shop and charge on. On December 7, 1966, I go with John Chirenza—a friend and fellow haircutter—and open a shop on Melrose Avenue (long before the street became fashionable) and name it the "Iron Flute" after an eleventh-century book of koans. We're both into the same thing, to have a kicked-back shop without the pompy bullshit. First thing we do is hang an antique hash pipe on the wall behind the reception counter, setting the tone of the shop and the times...

The first year is relentlessly bleak. I'm damn near broke. Have I made the right move? Fortunately, things begin to change for the better when Sue, a friend of Marilyn's, drops in (I can't remember her last name). She's a road manager for a new and unknown band out of Canada called Buffalo Springfield. Sue is totally jacked-up on the group, says they're going to be big stars—but at the moment they're low on bread and would I cut their hair for freebees because they have a photo shoot tomorrow and she'd really appreciate the gesture and will absolutely make it up to me when they become famous...I believe her.

Now I'm cutting Steven Stills, Graham Nash and Neil Young. Steven Stills: friendly, he has a laid-back lightness, not a trace of self importance, quick to laugh, no hassle with the cut. Graham Nash: shoes, nails and manners, all highly polished. Lots of eye contact. Neil Young: now here's a piece of work. He moves like a drunken praying mantis. He collapses his effete frame onto the cutting chair, all the time his head is bowed low, his chin stuck to his chest. Never once looking at his reflection in the mirror. Silent, deep into his own thoughts. I cut Neil's hair for a couple of years. In all that time, we never exchanged a full sentence.

For the first year, I'm graciously doing their hair, free-bees. Then Buffalo Springfield makes the big time. Sue keeps her word, pays me in full and highly recommends the shop to others in the biz. In a few months, business is booming, I'm building a prime clientele, no assholes. I'm now doing several groups.

With "The Band," it's usually a house call. I go to a big house in Malibu—complete with its own recording studio—and spend the entire day cutting their hair. They're rural, woodsy guys—except for Robbie Robertson, he's a gentle and sophisticated man. I cut Robbie for several years. Always a smile, unassuming, and he's a damn good guitar player.

"The Association's" music is pure vanilla. Russ Giguere and Ted Bluechel are half cool, the rest are flawless snobs. "Deep Purple"—Ritchie Blackmore, Dave Coverdale and the others—were for real. "America" and a few other bands were forgettable.

Some of my other regulars were: Charles Cowles of "Art Forum" magazine and a New York art gallery owner; Richard Kirsch, the critic/writer/columnist; Sidney Sheldon, the writer, was a pompous dink; Hal Blaine, superior drummer, good man; Morton Phillip—Okay—Morton...

I cut Morton's hair at Jay's shop for awhile, then lost contact with him when I did my stint with Elvis. I really didn't know much about him. He was middle-aged, and from his svelte frame hung finely tailored suits. He was refined, but not in-your-face refined, unassuming and generous. He would walk to his limo (he had a personal chauffeur) that was parked a block away from the shop. This man obviously did not want to shine in the spotlight. In the last year or so, we've had a few sociable evenings together—dinner, music. Wherever we'd go, he's rendered unfeigned deference. In all that time, I never asked him about his private life or his business affairs.

One day after cutting his hair, I'm saying goodbye to him at the front door. He splits. In my ear, my partner John asks, "Do you know who Morton is, man?"

"No. Who is he?"

"Heavy bucks, man."

"Like what?"

"He owns a few companies."

"Like what?"

Now we're walking through the shop, instinctively heading for our private outdoor smoking yard in the back of the shop, enclosed by a ten-foot high wooden fence. John strikes a doobie—we puff.

"So, what about the companies?" I ask.

"Can't remember that right now, man," says John through a veil of primo Oxaca smoke, "'cept Presto."

"Presto. Like Mandrake?"

"No, man, Presto. Like cooking ware."

"Presto cooking pots and pans, is that what you're saying?"

"What am I telling ya, man."

"Ey, cool...He's laid back." I'm looking up at a baby-blue and cloudless sky. Nice. The shop is doing well, I have a neat clientele, feeling good.

"More, man...Get this," coughs John.

"This another heavy number?"

"Ya', ready?"

"Carry on."

"Dig it. Abigail fuckin' Van Buren, man."

"Who?"

"Dear fuckin' Abby!"

"Ya' kidding?"

"For real. The broad has a zillion people fallin' for her rap. She's into answers, man. Ya' got a problem? She's got an answer. She's gotta have at least forty jerk-offs whacking on typewriters and shit, banging out all kinds of bullshit answers."

"The one on the phone with the crackly voice?"

"That's the broad."

"She always calls me Sally?"

"Dear fuckin' Abby, man."

"That's a strange hookup, man...Morton and Abby."

"Maybe she has something going on?"

"Right...Who knows?"

"What evil lurks in the mind of man? The Shadow knows. Radio number," says John.

"I remember...Remember 'The Whistler?'"

Intuitively, we whistle "The Whistler" theme song together as we wander back into the shop...Things are rolling along nicely...

A couple more weeks into my karma, I meet Abby. Beverly Hills Hotel. I'm there to do Morton's hair. A quick buzz on the door button. I wait...I dig moments like this. Doors...trippy...You never know who, or what, lies ahead on the other side of the door. Let's see...Curtain...The door slowly opens and I'm looking at a plain-Jane girl, mid-twenties, mousey hair, rumpled clothes—well maybe not rumpled—it just feels like her clothes should be rumpled.

"Hi. I'm Jenny, Morton's daughter." We shake hands—a grip with intense authority—I mumble through the amenities and settle down onto a squishy couch...Was it Jenny? Genie? Let's say Jenny. So Jenny offers me a glass of champagne. I politely decline. Morton enters the room. He's half dressed, looks weary and tense.

"Sal, have you met my daughter?"

"Indeed, I have," I cordially reply.

Morton turns to Jenny. "How's everything?" asks Morton, indicating the closed bedroom door.

"She's getting dressed," whispers Jenny.

Morton motions for me to follow him into the bathroom to cut his hair. In two minutes, I'm into it. Morton is tense and taciturn. Every five minutes or so, Jenny creaks open the closed bedroom door, peeks inside the room, checks it out, then gives Morton a quick bulletin on what's happening.

"My wife is a wonderful woman," says Morton, flat, like he was reading a gas bill.

I nod my head knowingly, get back into the haircut.

"We've been married for a long time, Sal," continues Morton stifling a deep sigh.

Suddenly, bam! Dear Ol' Abby comes blasting out of the bedroom like an errant rocket. Her hair (teased, lacquered, unmovable), layers of sparkling jewelry, and piles of makeup, all coming at you like a disgruntled water buffalo. After bouncing off the living room walls for a couple of minutes, she sticks her head into the bathroom and gives Morton an air-kiss. Then she turns to me all glittery, with a stiff-as-steel smile, and out of the corner of her mouth says, "Hi Sally. I'm Abby," she loudly proclaims.

In the next couple of years, I come to know her better. Okay. She's amped in the red zone—doggedly blunt, loud, but likeable. One time I asked her what the greatest aphrodisiac is for women? Without hesitation she belts out, "Money, Sally. Money!"

Six months later, two more talented hairdressers join us: Sal Valentino and Joe Vega. Josephina Pangrazio is our earthy receptionist, who glides around the shop in her bare feet like a butterfly. Italian-Americans all. The crew is kicked back and so are the clientele. Couple times a day—when the vibe is right—we lock the entrance door, then crew and clients alike gather in the smoking yard to spark a couple of joints—a quick puff, then we reenter the shop, grab a quido, or claves, maracas, whatever, off the walls, boost the volume, and play along with the music of Credence Clearwater, Santana, Herbie Mann, the Beatles, etc. After fifteen or twenty minutes of releasing energies, we settle down and get back to the hair thing.

The shop was definitely the place to find celebrities or about-to-become celebrities, much as Jay's shop had been a nexus for the famous. Alan Sherman was a client (the songwriter who wrote "Hello Mudda, Hello Fadda" as well as other tunes). Alan is soft in voice and body. I asked him why he thinks the song became such a hit. "Damn if I know," he says. "I was just fucking around, the next thing you know, I'm making money."

In the reception room, squatting on the floor, Dobie Grey is playing the guitar and singing a brand new song he's about to record. "Drift Away" sounds like nothing to me. No melody, no layers, silly shit, the tune will never make it, never be a hit. (Yeah, I know, I know).

Dennis Wilson of the Beach Boys is high spirited, chatty, friendly, picky about his hair. The thing is, it's hard for him to let go of a buck and it's the same story each time I cut his hair. "Oh, I forgot the bread, I'll get you next time." Bullshit. Right now he owes me a few hundred bucks for unpaid haircuts. But I like him. You can't help but like him. He's innocent...

Along with Loren Schwartz, a friend who's known Brian Wilson for years, I visit Brian at his house. Entering the house, you face a big living room, the floor of which is covered entirely in gritty sand. In one corner of the room resides a white grand piano, in the center of the room looms a large Arabian tent into which we enter. There's more sand on the floor and as we squat on colorful cushions, Loren introduces me to Brian.

Brian is distant, his speech is strained and staccato. He's gotta be on some exotic medication. And the sandy beach theme? What's next, a seaweed suit? It's gotta be the medication. Dig it. All the while Brian is talking, he's tossing a golf ball-sized rubber ball across the tented room, and this little bitsy pooch eagerly retrieves the ball and plops it back onto Brian's lap. Brian, while still talking to Loren, retosses the ball and, predictably, the little dog gleefully retrieves it and replops it onto Brian's sandy lap. That's how it goes, toss, retrieve, toss, retrieve, on and on, while a desultory conversation between Loren and Brian is going on.

Unpredictably, the dog decides to plop the ball onto my lap. At first I don't react, hoping the pooch will ignore me and get back to Brian. But the little guy will have none of that, nudging me with his cold snout as if to say, "Hey Buster, get busy, throw the ball." I try to tune in on the disjointed conversation between my friend and Brian, but it's impossible, the insistent canine will have his way. I relent and toss the ball across the Saharan floor. The dog flies into action, retrieves the ball and dumps it onto my lap. That's how it goes for the next half hour, me and the dog, toss and retrieve.

Brian doesn't seem to notice a thing between me and the dog, so I tune in on the dog's world and watch him zipping back and forth. To the dog, human speech sounds like hollow noises. One has to pay attention to separate the words distinctly, but that don't mean shit to the dog. He's blissed out hunting the ball, getting hold of it between his teeth and dumping it back onto my lap. All the while, Brian is into his own spacey trip, his blinking, vacant eyes unaware of the relentless dynamic between me and his dog. Never once did he offer us a cup of tea or a glass of water. Nothing. This guy is deeply absorbed in his own trip.

Another client is Jan Murray. Jan is a comedian from the old school. Vaudeville, television, Vegas. He's got that snappy patter down — pa da pa, pa da ping, and then she said, like that. The first time he comes into the shop, he takes one look at a huge abstract painting I've recently purchased which looks like some drunk has flung buckets of colorful paint onto the canvas. "What do you call it? Mother?" he quips.

While getting his haircut, he'll run through a few jokes or bits of his standup routine, keenly gauging the response from the folks in the shop. To me, under his breath, he'll say, "A, B, B minus," etc. Once in awhile, he'll sink deeply into the cutting chair and in a soft intimate voice bemoan life's travails, or lay a sad-ass tear-jerking story on me about his uncle dying, or how his dog has measles. Even then, I expect him to pop into his usual peppy patter. He's sad? He's happy? What? Someone said, the under-planking of humor is tragedy. It figures, the thing with the theater mask.

When I was in Vegas one weekend, I ran into Jan at the Sahara Hotel where he was appearing. He was alone, sitting at a table in the casino bar, sipping on a tall drink with a teensy umbrella hanging on the rim of the glass. He motions for me to join him. I do. Do I want a drink? he asks. I nay the drink. He beckons the waitress—calls her honey— asks for more ice for his drink, and maybe a taller glass. He's tapping his fingers on the tabletop, he's nervous. He's usually garrulous—tonight he's uncharacteristically laconic. "What a business," he says wearily.

"You love it."

"Like you cutting hair?"

"Some days I don't mind it at all."

"A rabbi, I should be."

"The world can use a funny rabbi."

The waitress returns, places our drinks on the table. "How's the crowd in the lounge?" Jan asks her.

"So so," she answers.

"Stiff?" he further probes.

"Not bad," she says as she turns to leave.

Jan sighs, checks his watch. "I gotta go. See ya after the show," he says gulping down his drink. He splits, and I head for the Lounge Room.

Before I can spot an empty table, I hear Sonny West's drawling voice call, "Hey Saul." I turn and see Elvis and a few of the Guys sitting at a long table across the room. Sonny waves for me to join them. At the table, everyone is in a festive mode—I find out Elvis and the Guys are in town strictly for pussy playtime. Face it—the King has a wary eye. Elvis asks, "How y'all doing?"

"Good, everything's cool," I answer.

The King looks good—laughing and jiving with his Guys. That I miss. The southern jive-ass banter, it's special, one day it will no longer be. Gone...Thus they carry on for a few minutes, until the lights dim and an offstage announcer introduces Jan Murray. Out strolls Jan, nonchalant but full of upwelling energy. He gets right into his routine—quick, witty, urbane stuff. We're all laughing, it's a joy to see a pro in action. Halfway through his routine, he stops and announces to the folks that Elvis Presley is in the audience. Applause. Applause. A spotlight hits our table. Elvis quickly sets down his drink—probably ginger ale—and eases to a standing position. He's a star now. He smiles his starry smile, bows his starry head, waves his starry wave, then slowly descends back onto his chair—more implicitly, his "country boy" chair. Back to jiving with his Guys.

After the show is over, Jan joins us at our table. I introduce Jan to Elvis and the Guys. Elvis is cordial, we chat for a few minutes, until he gets up to leave, but not before asking me if I would like to tag along with him and the Gang. I respectfully decline. They leave. I'm standing beside Jan...

"So you know Elvis," says Jan.

"Kinda," I vaguely reply.

David Geffen's first words to me were, "Can you cut Jewish hair?" At the time he was in partnership with Bones Howe and Pat Colecio managing a couple of up-and-coming bands and singers. Bones, a client, recommended David to me. I'm always a bit apprehensive when I'm doing someone new. I work hard at avoiding stressful people. If our egos clash, it's over. If my mind don't groove, my fingers won't move. David arrived for his appointment exactly on time. He's a notch below medium height, a few years younger than me, has a thatch of brown curly hair, and he smells clean and soapy.

Six haircuts down the line—sometimes in the shop, sometimes at his Malibu Beach house—I'm getting down with the man. He's swift, bright and cunning, and he expertly plays the naive role with people. "Oh really. What does that mean?" he would ask. He damn well knows exactly what something means or doesn't mean. He does a few more "Oh, really's"—then Pow!—he slams you, like a rock on a raisin. He's a swift motherfucker. As yet, I haven't seen a shadow of mendacity cross his boyish face—what he says, he means. I like him. He's a real guy.

It's 1968. Another year has zoomed by...Charlie Hodge, Joe Esposito, Red and Sonny West, Lance Lagault and a few more of Elvis' Guys frequent the shop—they keep me up to date on the King's karma.

I learn that Larry Geller and Colonel Tom Parker are definitely not grooving. The Colonel believes that Larry is stirring up all kinds of weird metaphysical stuff in Elvis' vulnerable head. He wants Larry out.

Elvis wants Larry in. So that's happening. Heavy, bad vibes. The Colonel is hooked up with some powerful juice in this country, one phone call and he could have Larry grounded to fine powder in an hour. I hope Larry knows what the hell he's into with the old man.

I haven't seen Elvis for over a year. Steve Binder—a client—is producing an Elvis "comeback" special for NBC. It will be a live performance, the setting a boxing ring. The only bummer is the Colonel. He's a real pain in the ass, Steve goes on to say. He ignores the Colonel's dumb suggestions because Elvis is on Steve's side and that's what really matters. On the show that was broadcast, Elvis wore a tight black leather suit. He paced around the "ring" for a few minutes, then sat down with a few of his buddies and a couple of guitars—he sang, they reminisced. Elvis never looked better.

It's late afternoon, the shop is jammed. Credence Clearwater's music dominates the scene—that is, until Elvis casually walks in. Man, he's an eyeful—bedecked to his eyelashes in black, with gold bracelets and chains dangling from his wrists, sparkling diamonds on each of his twitchy fingers, a long flowing Dracula cape, all this dramatically garnished with a slim, silvery cane.

Elvis greets me warmly, ameliorating any suspicion that he might be pissed off at me for quitting the gig. I give him a quick tour of the shop. For a couple of minutes, people don't recognize him. Then it's— "Is that who I think it is?" "Looks like him." It hits them. It's Elvis! The shop soars. The King smiles and jokes with the flashing folk. After ten minutes, he's had enough. I escort him to his limo in front of the shop. The Guys, Richard, Allen and Joe are standing in a "parade rest" position—they snap to attention as Elvis, using his cane like a baton, gives them a downbeat.

"At ease, men," says the King to his faithful minion, and the Guys drop the military bullshit. There are handshakes, a hug or two, then we all climb into the limo, split a couple of Pepsis and drum up a few memories. After a few minutes of friendly reminiscing, I remember that I left a client sitting in my chair. I do a hasty goodbye to the King and crawl out of the limo. The sunroof rolls back then, standing up, shaking and waving his shiny cane, the King shouts, "Charge, you fucker! Charge!" A screechy U-turn and he's gone...

Right now I feel, well, like I'm part of the Hollywood scene. Come on, the King casually dropping by the shop to say hello. I'm kinda proud...Wow! I can't believe I just said that. What bullshit. Elvis is another human being, stuck in "the world of ten thousand things" like the rest of us. Man, this Hollywood thing is getting to me...

I sense a change in my life. A big change. Every time I sense a change, it happens. I should invest in a crystal ball or something, go occult. Damn right. "Charge you fucker, charge!" Live life straight on. Sempre Avanti!

❧

It's a few months down the road—I'm putting the finishing touches on a client's hair when I hear, "Happy birthday, man." The soft voice is Jay's. I turn around, check him out—he looks rumply and tired, yet his eyes are clear and bright. It's a kiss on each cheek and a firm hug. He's grinning, he wants to tell me something. I bid goodbye to my client—Jay knows the guy. They do a couple of quick "hi's and how are ya's?" Done. I indicate the back of the shop—Jay nods yes. We head for the backyard, Jay spots the bathroom, holds up one finger, indicating one minute. I point to the backyard, he nods yes, slips into the bathroom.

I gotta tell you. In the bathroom, hanging on the wall, there is a rectangular frame about the size of Time magazine. On the frame are the words "TIME Man Of The Year." The thing is, you have to look real close to see who it is. So you place your face close to the frame and what you see is—your own reflection. It's a mirror. So that's the bit.

A couple minutes later, Jay joins me in the backyard. He's chortling hard and wiping tears from his eyes. In a blink, I'm laugh-riffing right along with him.

"Your face looking right back at you," Jay guffaws.

We settle down. Jay is staring hard at me. "I like your shop, man. It's together. I hear you're doing well," says Jay.

"It's getting better, man."

Jay continues staring and smiling at me. "What's with the eyeballs, man?" I ask.

"I just got off a plane from New York. I thought about you, man...I miss you."

"Life's vicissitudes...I miss you too, man."

"Yeah, vicissitudes..." says Jay with a facile smile.

"What's going on? Tell me."

"You ready?"

"Wha'cha got?"

"I'm getting into another bag."

"Like what?"

"Like it's time to expand. Open new shops—here, New York, Europe, Italy, fucking Rome. Cosmetics, shampoo, charm school for men, the whole trip."

"No shit?"

"Gospel, man."

"Great."

"Yeah, it is. That's why I want you to carry some of the load."

"What will I do?"

"Help me make decisions. Psyche me out. You'll be my advisor. Man, we fly around, check out the world. Happy birthday!" Jay hands me a silver roach-holder. "Dig the abstract design," he says, "no two alike, the guy makes them by hand."

"Grazie, amico mio."

"Prego. Man, I gotta go. Come up to the house. We'll talk. Sharon always asks about you. Call me. Rome, my man, Rome!"

Jay rips away from the curb in a nifty Porsche. He's got my head buzzing. Should I sell the shop? Keep it? What's ahead? Look at me, I'm actually trying to figure out what the future will bring? It's a waste of time. I know that. Still, I have these prescient flashes. It's like a knee-jerk reaction thing. Is this the change I've been expecting?

The next day at the shop I'm soaking up the sunshine in the backyard. On my portable radio, Bob Dylan is lamenting about his Lady Love. The melancholy music is unceremoniously interrupted by an announcement. "Mass murder in Beverly Hills. Five people brutally stabbed and shot to death. Sharon Tate, Jay Sebring, Abigail Folger—" the announcer's voice continues on—I no longer hear it.

Two phones ring simultaneously. I answer—someone is crying on the phone. I hang up. I feel queasy—head for the restroom. At the sink, after dousing my face and neck with cold water, I look up and into the "Man Of The Year" mirror and hear Jay's jubilant voice echoing, "Rome, my man, Rome!"

What happened? Why? Who committed the murders? All kinds of theories and rumors are bouncing around Hollywood. Jay and Sharon were into an occult thing? A dope deal gone wrong? A revenge thing against Jay? Hollywood is into some serious paranoia. The police are questioning anyone who knew Jay or Sharon. I'm in Jay's address book. It's just a matter of time before the police get to me. That day happens two months later.

He's waiting for me when I arrive at the shop for a day of hair snipping. Stocky, puffy eyes, a washable blue suit, mid-forties. A cop? He asks me if he can talk to me about Jay Sebring. I suggest the back of the shop. I step aside, indicate the way. We head for the backyard. His eyes are wide open, taking in every inch of the shop. In the backyard— we face each other.

"My name is Miles Hebding," he says handing me his card.

"A cop?"

"Insurance."

"I don't need insurance."

"No, I investigate life insurance claims. Jay Sebring has a policy with us. It's double indemnity, which amounts to a substantial sum of money."

"Like, how much?"

"I'm not at liberty to reveal the amount of money," he says as he eyes the backyard. He looks amused. Then back to me. "You and Sebring were friends?"

I ignore his question. "How did you find me? The police never did."

"The police called your cousin, who has the same name as you. Over the phone, someone told the police that he was on location shooting a movie in Arizona. They never checked further. Mind if I ask you a few questions?"

Who the hell is this guy? Does he think Jay was murdered for the insurance money?

"Look, Mr. Hebding—"

"Miles."

"Miles. Nobody knows shit, right? Who did it? Why? Police don't know. Could be anybody. It could be you, for all I know. Right?"

"Right."

"So, I'm wary answering any questions about Jay and Sharon, unless I'm sure about the person I'm talking to. Can you dig that?"

"Absolutely. Fine. You have my card. Check me out. I'll call you in a few days. Thank you for your time."

A couple of well-placed phone calls and I learn that Miles Hebding is for real. He's a high ranking investigator, handles the big buck claims. I was further informed not to be deceived by his cherubic demeanor.

A week later, Miles calls. I tell him everything is cool—he books an appointment for a haircut. The following day, he plunks into my cutting chair, he's bright and ready. He looks straight into the mirror as I cut his attenuated locks. "Mind answering a few questions while you cut my hair?"

"I'm here."

"How long did you know Jay Sebring?"

"'Bout eight years."

"How did you meet him?"

"I auditioned for a job."

"To cut hair?"

"Right."

"Really?"

"Really."

"So, when you were no longer working for him, where did you go next?"

"I did one person's hair. Exclusively. Lived and traveled with him."

"Nobody else?"

"Right."

"Really?"

"Really."

"Who is this person?"

"Elvis Presley."

Miles is looking deep into my eyes searching for the slightest trace of bullshit.

"Really?"

"Really. Look Miles, do you want to know about Jay or me?"

"Well, that's damn interesting that you did that. Okay. What about Sebring, what kind of a man was he?"

I don't know what the hell to say about Jay. How do I define him? Bright, feisty, meticulous, impulsive? The most unprejudiced man I have ever known? How everything with him has to be accurate, factual, down to the last tiny detail? How he lived his life, like a fluent novel? How existentially hip he was? How he changed the business of men haircutting? I rattle off a few prosaic verities about Jay, enough to get me through the drill. When I mention the martial arts thing with Ed Parker and Bruce Lee—he abruptly interrupts me.

"Jay was stabbed and shot. You would think, with all that martial arts skill, that he would try and protect himself."

"Huh?"

"Like grab a pillow or a blanket or something, wrap it around his arm for protection from whoever is wielding the knife."

"I don't know. Maybe he was thinking about Sharon's well-being, and went along with the scenario thinking the assailant or assailants weren't murderers. Shit, I don't know, man."

Miles seems satisfied with my answers. He peers at his image in the mirror—pats his hair. "Great haircut." He thanks me for taking time to answer his questions and leaves. I never see or hear from him again.

CHAPTER TEN

I'm holding onto a delicate crystal glass. Hold it too tight, it will shatter. Too loose, it will fall to the ground. Once again, life's many vicissitudes manifest—I'll get right to it. Marilyn split. Hooked up with a musician—a drummer, a black guy, Maurice White—that's got to be an oxymoron. Don't mean shit to me, black, white, blue, we're all fucked up. Anyhow, our soul mate thing went south. I feel lower than whale scat. I've been dumped...Who needs the usual pedestrian paradigm, marriage, kids? It's become a moribund lifestyle.

Herman Hesse, Alan Watts, D.T. Susuki, R.H. Blythe. I'm mind tripping. What are we? What's a we? What's life? Death? I'm smothered in paradox. I've had a couple of dandy satoris, an epiphany or two, and I've come to realize that I don't know shit. All along, Marilyn had been with me—two weavers weaving the same self-probing cloth. Now alone, I'm sitting in our defunct cottage—it's a ball-breaking reality, and I'm feeling sorry for myself.

Seven A.M. Plane wheels screech, smacking the steamy airport runway. Las Vegas. Smouldering hot. Joe Esposito called and asked if I wouldn't mind coming to Las Vegas to do Elvis' hair for his opening show at the International Hotel. He would take care of accommodations. Sounds good. I'm looking forward to seeing Elvis perform in front of a live audience. For me, it's always been on a studio set or recording studio or a few deft moves at Graceland.

Later in the afternoon, after an icy cold shower and a couple hours sleep, I dutifully ascend to the King's penthouse. The joint is jumping. A party. Singers, musicians, a few actors, and as always three or four of Elvis' Guys. I mingle, sipping on a glass of chardonnay, checking out the scene. I literally bump into Sonny West—we rap for a few minutes. I find Sonny infinitely easy to talk to. He channeled me into the exclusive world of Elvis Presley and showbiz. We have a special bond between us.

A half hour into the scene, Elvis emerges from, I strongly suspect, his sub-zero temperature bedroom. He greets me with a warm smile and a iron-hard handshake, asks if I wouldn't mind doing his hair tonight just before the show? I assure him that I will be ready at his convenience. Elvis sticks around for a few minutes, then retreats to his glacial quarters. I hang around a while longer checking out the room. These are "special people," special because, to whatever degree, they know Elvis Presley. Hey, that includes me. Thing is, I don't feel special. I feel like I'm in a three-ring circus and I'm the schmuck selling peanuts.

It's evening, I'm trailing Jerry Schilling through a labyrinth of backstage corridors, passing boisterous kitchens, money-counting rooms, wardrobe rooms, etc. Ultimately we end up at Elvis' dressing room, in front of which a burly security guard stands squarely. He gives me a squinty once-over. "He's a friend," says Jerry to the flawlessly uncharismatic guard. A couple of taps on the door, and we're in.

The room is Las Vegas glitzy-plush, with a mirrored horseshoe bar. A quick pan of the room. Mostly family. Vernon Presley, his wife, Colonel Tom Parker. I do my polite and humble routine—it's a faux-friendly greeting I get in return. Hey, I'm happy. You never know in showbiz; one day you're in, another day you're way the fuck out. Jerry directs me to an adjacent room in which Elvis, half dressed, is waiting for me. Jerry leaves the room.

"Will you have time to do my hair, man?" Elvis asks in a low monotone voice.

"How much time?"

"'Bout...soon." Charlie slips into the room. "How much time?" Elvis asks Charlie.

"Half an hour. You have to get dressed too," says Charlie, calm and discreet.

"Can you do it, Sal?" asks Elvis.

"Nothing to it," I reply with bogus confidence.

Elvis sits down in front of the dressing room mirror. He checks out his image, then indicates the back of his head. "Something not together back there, man."

"Red or blue?" asks Charlie holding up two shirts.

"Blue," mumbles Elvis.

"We don't have much time, Elvis," Charlie gingerly adds as he leaves the room.

"Sal. Hit it," says Elvis.

I get to it. Elvis closes his eyes—I can feel him pulling away from me, going deeper into his own world. After fifteen minutes of meditative silence, it's a wrap. Elvis slowly opens his eyes and stares blankly at his reflected image. With his hand he feels the back of his head. "Got it," says Elvis, pleased with my tonsorial chops.

"Looks right, man."

"Thanks, man. Charlie..."

"I'll get him."

I quickly pack my hair gear and return to the horseshoe barroom and inform Charlie that he's needed. That deed done, I settle down at the bar. Somebody pours me a bracing shot of scotch, which I down in one indiscreet gulp. Two scotches into it, Elvis' door swings open and there he is, fully decorated in his stage regalia. He extends his fingers, shakes them, a quick scan of the room, and then it's "Let's go."

Joe Esposito, Sonny West, Charlie, two guards, a couple of hotel executives and myself follow Elvis through the twisting corridors, only it's a lot different this time. The usual backstage cacophony ceases when Elvis passes by. Everybody, but everybody, stops what they're doing to say hello and reverently acknowledge his royal presence with wide-eyed adoration. Elvis waves and jokes with the people as we worm our way to the theater. A few more twisty turns and we're backstage.

Backstage is the underbelly—a special world where you see the brothers and sisters of performance hovering around the starting curtain like frisky thoroughbreds anxious to run. I break off from Elvis' posse and head for my reserved primo booth to see the show.

First, it's a low rumble, like an inchoate earthquake, which slowly builds in intensity—louder, faster, then bam! Richard Strauss' "Thus Spake Zarathustra" (the theme to "2001: A Space Odyssey") fills the room, feeding the excitement, building anticipation. A cymbal clash, a pause, then an announcer's deep voice says, "Ladies and gentleman, Elvis Presley."

A tight spotlight covers Elvis as he confidently strides onto stage. The applause is third-rail electric. Elvis jumps right into it. The orchestra is burning, as well they should, for this is the "King of Rock and Roll." I could heap all kinds of praise about his performance—I'll do it with one word—Great! The man gives all. He absolutely has his shit together.

In his dressing room after the show, the room is overflowing with show folk. Making my way through the crush of famous faces, I run into Sammy Davis, Jr.

"Yeah, how ya been, man?" he says. "Heard you're with Elvis."

"I'm cool. I'm no longer with him. Well, occasionally I do his hair."

"He's a great artist, man."

"So are you, man."

"You're smooth, man. Motherfucker got a platinum tongue."

We laugh. I spot an empty seat at the bar, bid Sammy adios, and pounce on the stool. Sammy is for real. Once you get by that in-your-face-wide-as-the-Mississippi-River smile, there's a homegrown real person.

After a few minutes, Elvis emerges from his dressing room, comes over to where I'm sitting and asks for a glass of ice water. I offer him my bar stool. He declines, says he'd rather stand. In half a minute, Tom Jones is at his side. He's respectful and blatantly impressed with Elvis. Well, is it real? It's hard to say with the showbiz folk, they have sycophancy down to an art. I'm not saying that Mr. Jones is obsequious, not overtly anyway—although when he shook Elvis' hand, his eyes went all wide and lingering like he just spotted the Pope in the men's room taking a piss. Elvis introduces me to Mr. Jones, who gives me a textbook showbiz smile as he looks me over assessing my puny persona. Is he somebody? He looks familiar. He must be somebody, he's with Elvis. His eyes say that I'm a "maybe."

I'm growing appreciably less than enraptured with haircutting. I sell my half of the shop to my partner John Chirenza and migrate to Big Sur, California and settle into a rustic cabin deep into Polo Colorado Canyon. It has two huge fireplaces, a long front porch overlooking the verdant forest, and beyond that the boundless blue ocean—plus a thriving vegetable garden. I'm ready to kick back, let my hair grow down to my shoulders and take stock of my karma.

I have my day-to-day program down. After an early morning breakfast and spiking my orange juice with a taste of mescaline, it's a long enlightening walk in the forest. In the afternoon, I pedal my new bike down the highway a few miles to Esalen (a psychological studies institute) and hook up with all kinds of folk who are into self-awareness. Hot, steamy outdoor baths, primo smoke, plenty of pussy (I know, I shouldn't say pussy, it just comes out that way). I'm slowly coming down from my ego-shattering experience. I've made mistakes. I'm learning.

I survive by doing house calls for a few "highliners." Very fortunately, I get top bucks for my haircutting skills—whatever they may be—enabling me to roll along with the "eternal moment."

One of those "house calls" has taken me to New York City. I'm in the Pierre Hotel, about eight hundred stories up, gazing out the window at always vibrant Manhattan. Art, music, books, museums, theater, buses, taxis, subways, honks, beeps, rattles, whistles—Manhattan. I love it.

I'm in David Geffen's swanky suite. David has been on a unrelenting rant for the last hour. Could be about anything—losing a big deal, a dirty ashtray. Right now his jugular veins are popping, he's screaming at Linda, his personal secretary. I've known David for a few years now, I'm familiar with his volatile outbursts. David is now a big kahuna in showbiz, a billionaire. After having cursed the universe with vengeful ire, his anger subsides and, like a snake in a sack, he settles down ready to have his haircut. I snip, we chat, not a word about his bratty behavior. After an hour, done. I go back to my hotel.

I stick around the City for a couple of days, get my culture fix, then it's back to Big Sur. Back to singing birds, whispering winds, the yellow sway of grassy meadows—at nighttime a symphony of cacophonous insects. I'm home.

Two years pass. Reluctantly, I leave my rural haven and head back to Hollywood. Heavy with angst, I have absolutely no desire to cut hair. However, that doesn't mean shit. I'm keenly bereft of coin, I've gotta get my act together, pronto. I feel like jumping into a gopher hole.

After six months of anxious scuffling, I manage to put together a small shop in Beverly Hills. It's a modest second-story room directly across the street from the famous Nate and Al's deli on Beverly Drive. Looking out from my shop window, I view a daily parade of the Hollywood hierarchy: directors, writers, movie stars, all frequenters of the restaurant. Art Carney usually shows up before noon, hot-footing it inside, his long arms swinging like a Gibbon ape. I catch Yul Brynner climbing out of his Mercedes roadster (his world-famous golden pate shining like polished brass) with charming smiles for everyone.

Groucho Marx, another regular at Nate and Al's, is in bad shape. Feeble, skeletal, glassy-eyed—assisted by his chauffeur and what I gather to be his male nurse. I watch him struggle painfully trying to get out of his limo and stand on his own two feet. Miraculously, he does. Assisted by his two guys, he inches his way across the street, shuffling like a wounded iguana, then painfully straightens up and enters the restaurant like an effete warrior...

Broderick Crawford—remember him? Big tough, gravel-voiced, in-your-face guy. Now he's shrunken, like a raisin. These are a few of the awesome icons I grew up with. Decaying now. We're all in this dream together, us Homo Sapiens: we're here, and then, we're not.

✑

Joe calls me, asks if I could do Elvis' hair. Once again I'm winding up Sunset Canyon. Inside the house, Marty Laker, Joe and I rap for a few minutes. Elvis joins us, casually dressed, nothing stagey. He's anxious about something, I feel his anticipation. He motions for me to follow him. I break off from Joe and Marty and follow Elvis, padding through a semi-lit hallway, at the end of which is a small nursery room complete with crib and a six-month old infant. For a couple of minutes we remain mute, checking out the baby.

"Hard to believe, man," I say, softly.

"Li'l-bitty thing," says Elvis tenderly touching the baby's hands.

"Boy?"

"Girl."

"I'm sorry, man. I heard that you had a baby, I didn't catch whether it was a boy or girl. Either way, it's great. Great."

"Li'l-bitty thing can change a man's life," says Elvis leaning in closer to the baby.

"For sure. What's her name?"

"Lisa Marie," say Elvis, his chest swelling with fatherly pride. After a couple of minutes of silently observing Lisa Marie, Elvis asks, "My hair, man?"

"My pleasure."

I do his hair. He really doesn't need a trim, I figure he wanted to show me his baby. The haircut was just his way of doing it. After the haircut, I hang around for a couple of hours, laid back on a long serpentine sofa, rapping with the King. He's genuinely concerned about my well being. He asks if I need anything? Is everything alright? I assure him that everything is just dandy. I pick up that if I wanted to come back to work for him, the gig is open. Then he leaves the room. I'm alone. Where is everyone? The friendly bantering between the Guys? It's quiet, still. No music. Things are different, the ol' vicissitudes action again. With the baby and all, things have changed. Flat-ass dull changes.

In a few minutes, Elvis returns touting a couple of shiny pistols, which he reverently fingers as he sits next to me and eagerly launches into profound gun-speak—it's weight, balance, power, etc. Endlessly he does drone. I don't know shit about guns, and I'm certainly not comfortable being in spitting distance of firearms. I play the onlooker for a few minutes, then conveniently remember that I have a previous engagement and say goodbye to the King.

A year goes by. It happens. Elvis dies. Time stops, like a broken watch. A magnificent talent is gone...

He was never satisfied. A dissatisfaction with himself wore him down. At first, it was the easiest thing in the world. They set him up as a King. He felt like a cheat discovering a way to make it easy. His inner dissatisfaction rankled. Still, he entrusted his bloated body to bending over, his arms outstretched shaking the hands of adoring ladies. But he was tired. Thus he lived for years with small intervals of recuperation, in visible glory, honored by the world, his spirit deeply troubled—and more and more troubled, because no one was taking his troubles seriously. He, in a half-fainting trance and to the adulation of his public, surrounded himself with cheerful patter, distracting himself from himself. Except at night, when the hungry spectators faded away and no one was left except himself. Then it was different. Then it was real.

I'm old enough to have watched a few people pass through death's door. If I'm ever going to live my life the way I want to live my life, I had better get going now. Immediately. This nanosecond. I quit cutting hair and drop everyone, including my highliners, and get the hell out of the hair business for real. I trek back to the Monterey Peninsula. I rent a cozy cottage along Highway One. Adjacent to my driveway, about twenty feet away, is another driveway leading uphill to the world famous Carmel Highlands Inn. The Inn is set high on a bluff overlooking the voluminous Pacific Ocean, an ocean that hammers you into the "oneness" of existence. Sounds heavy, huh? I didn't mean for it to come off that way, but it did, so fuck it. After a couple of weeks of staring at the mesmerizing sea, I've decided to try writing.

Let me tell you about that. When I first arrived, I didn't have any direction, no explanations to myself about myself. My mind wandered free form. One day it felt like a guy yanking on my arm urging me to follow him, and I do, to a blank sheet of paper and a new ballpoint pen in my hand. The instant the ink hit the paper, it was like unclogging a sink drain, stuff started flowing, and it felt natural exploring my mind as I used to do when I was a kid.

Each morning, rain or shine, backpacked and penned, I truck on down the highway to the most beautiful place in the World—Point Lobos State Park. I'm almost reluctant to mention the name of the park, lest every asshole in the world comes here and mangles the shit out of its pristine beauty. I've discovered a perfect spot with the right "vibe" happening, on a cliff overlooking the turquoise ocean—with seals, otters, cormorants, seagulls, and with waves dramatically smashing against the sides of the rocky cliff dispersing sprays of salt water, refreshing my face and mind. I sound heavy, huh? I can't help it. This fucking ocean does that to me.

I'm pedaling my now beat-up bicycle down Carmel Valley Road. I'm about ten miles deep into the rural valley. It's a sunshiny, optimum day. I'm thinking about the characters in my play. It's a play about Italian-Americans, something I definitely know something about. Unconsciously, I turn off onto a side road. Hey, upper-class layout here. Big houses, big bucks, well-tended lawns and shrubbery, long driveways. The good life.

Ahead of me about a hundred feet away, I spot a sleek Mercedes sedan slowly rolling down a driveway onto the road on which I'm nonchalantly pedaling. What ho! It's Marilyn! My ball-breaking soul mate. Pain and Joy remembered at the same time. I duck my head low, hoping she hasn't seen me as I pump hard away from the scene. The Mercedes guns by me. I get a quick peek at the past. Earth, Wind and Fire is big time. She's living large. I have about twelve bucks...You see, it's irony that makes a writer a writer. That's what I have to figure—or else I would never get a good night's sleep.

After a hard day of scribbling at the park, it's back to my bungalow, a short nap and a quick shower, then a schlepp up the twisty Carmel Highlands driveway for food and drink. I hang for an hour or so listening to a seasoned jazz pianist doing his thing. After three scotches, I trudge down the driveway and in two minutes I'm in bed. No hardcore gung-ho cops nailing my ass. It's simple, just the way I like it.

A few months later, the play is finished and it's back to Hollywood. I'm pumped and ready to roll, anxious to see the play performed on stage. I'll cop out—I don't know if the play is good, bad, funny, sad? However, I'm unwaveringly determined to see it through. Am I a playwright or not? There's only one way to find out. Do it myself. Fuck all the schlepping around the city trying to find someone to produce it. I would be wasting my time. An unknown playwright? Forget it. People know me as a "men's hairdresser," a barber. That's like saying your submental. I'll produce the play myself. True, it will tap me out, but I've got to see the play on the boards.

Through a friend, I meet the great old-time character actor Vitto Scotti. He's been in hundreds of movies and he knows what he's talking about. I ask him if he would direct my play. Vitto says he can't do it, he has prior commitments, but he strongly suggests John Meyhers. I tell Vitto that I prefer everyone in the play, including the director, to be an Italian-American. Vitto looks me straight in the eye and informs me that I would be damn lucky to get Meyhers to direct the play, and if by chance I do, I would be getting a brilliant man, a man who knows more about Italians than anyone I'll ever meet. Vitto goes on to say that John Meyhers is an Italianophile, and repeats that I would be damn lucky if he would agree to direct my play.

A couple of days later, once again I'm motoring up Sunset Canyon Drive, looking for John Meyher's house. I find it. It's an Italian villa type, with steep steps leading to a massive, burnished wood door flanked by two squatting lion statues. After counting the eighteen steps leading to the door, I'm about to ring the bell, when it slowly opens. There he is.

It's a familiar face, which at the moment I cannot place. He's in his mid-sixties, with an effulgent smile, and radiating megawatt energy. He introduces himself and indicates for me to enter his home. I respectfully decline and hand him the manuscript of the play. He assures me that he will read it right away. I thank him and split.

It takes me about an hour to get back to my apartment. From the hallway I can hear my phone impatiently ringing. With much haste, I open the door and pounce on the phone.

"Salvatore?" a voice booms in my ear, pronouncing every syllable.

"Yes. Mr. Meyhers?"

"John. Call me John. Top notch, Salvatore."

"What's that?"

"Your play. First-class writing."

"You're kidding? You read the play already?"

"Every page. Absolutely wonderful, Salvatore."

"Well, thank you," I reply in my best sangfroid voice.

"Salvatore. Tomorrow. Breakfast at my house. Ten-o'clock." Bink! He hangs up. Wow. This cat is rolling. What the hell was that all about? Is this guy for real? The praise, the flattery? Still, it's reassuring to hear something positive about my writing.

The following morning, I'm counting the eighteen steps leading to his door. Once again, before I have a chance to ring the doorbell, the door swings open. There he is, arms outstretched ready to embrace me, which he does with much gusto. "My playwright," he proudly proclaims, "I'm hungry. Let's eat."

At the kitchen table, he introduces me to his beautiful actress wife, Joan Benedict, twenty years younger than himself. She humbly ladles out the breakfast fare. Halfway through the eggs and salmon, he tells me about the time he lived in Italy for twelve years. It seems that he was standing on a crowded street corner in Rome, when two American tourists asked him—in a pitiful attempt at speaking Italian—where a particular street was located. So, rattling on in Italian, he tells them the way to their destination. Naturally, they don't understand a word he's saying. Now he tries a combination of Italian and sign language, trying to communicate with the frustrated couple. Nada. Not a word do they understand. Suddenly he breaks out laughing. They are puzzled. "For God's sake, Salvatore, I forgot that I can speak English! Now I tell them in English and we all have a good laugh." I figure it's his way of telling me he knows Italian people and that he's qualified.

After the tasty breakfast, we retire to his study and settle down to business. He extols my play, wants to know how long I've been writing? Where was I educated? How many plays have I written? I tell him that I haven't been writing for long and that this is my first play. He's impressed—he urges me to stay away from the Hollywood writers and do my own thing. What about my background? My education? I tell him that after the play runs for a couple of weeks, I will reveal my background and my education. He squints his eyes curiously, then grins and says, "Fucking perfect."

The bell chimes. By the third chime, Joan answers the door. I hear light and tentative footsteps. Enter Tim Conway.

"Salvatore, meet Tim," clips John. "Salvatore is a brilliant new playwright."

"Zat so," Tim politely mutters.

I'm ready to split, as it looks like they have some business to take care of. John asks me to stick around. I do. John and Tim talk about a script they're writing together. I'm sipping on a glass of cold Chardonnay, listening to them talking about the script. It's obvious who's the teacher and who's the pupil. Tim is hanging onto every word that John is saying. No big ego thing with Mr. Conway, he's a rapt listener and eagerly wants to learn. He talks straight to you, no "I'm Tim Conway" bullshit.

An hour passes, Tim splits, now it's back to the nose-to-nose questioning about my play. John's questions and viewpoints about the play are keenly incisive. Later in the afternoon it's time to leave, but before I do I casually ask about his credits. "Ah, yes, of course, will do." That said, he scurries into another room, returns in two minutes and hands me his resume.

In my car, at stoplights, I peruse his resume. Get this. He's an actor and a writer. He's a Ph.D. He cofounded the Rome Theater Guild and the Rome Playhouse. He's a Broadway actor\singer, did "The Sound of Music" with Florence Henderson, played opposite Katherine Hepburn in "Anthony and Cleopatra," and was cast in "A Man For All Seasons" and "Camelot." He's directed numerous Broadway plays and musicals and, of course, Shakespeare. He's done over a hundred motion pictures and costarred with Bob Hope in "The Private Navy Of Sergeant O'Farrell." The list goes on—

But what really struck me was the part about him being a regular guest on the Jack Parr show. Now I remembered where I'd seen his face. Jack Parr had all these great, intelligent and fascinating people on his show, one of which was John Meyhers! I vividly remember Jack introducing John as the most brilliant and cultured person he has ever known. Then John would bow humbly to Jack and to the audience, sit down and merrily roll along about painting, sculpture, literature, music, whatever. By the time I got back to my apartment, I knew I was into some heavy company.

No second-rate stuff here. With John's help and his years of experience in the business, it wasn't difficult to find actors to do the play. I'm real lucky the way things come together. Among his choice for the cast was Frank de Kova—who has appeared in over seventy feature films and three hundred television shows—yet he is most recognizable for his continuing role of "Chief Wild Eagle" in "F Troop." He taught English at Columbia University, then turned to the professional stage. He starred on Broadway in "Detective Story" before Elia Kazan brought him to Hollywood for "Viva Zapata."

Also cast was Anthony Caruso, one of filmdom's finest character actors, with over two hundred films to his credit, including "Johnny Apollo" and "The Asphalt Jungle." He's played the tough gangster, the brave Indian Chief, plus numerous character roles. He was also the Honorary Mayor of Brentwood. We were also privileged to have aboard the consummate actor Al Ruscio, Gloria Manos, John Miranda and Peter Schrum. Save one (Tony Bova), all are seasoned actors.

I rent a rehearsal hall across the street from the famous Grauman's Chinese Theater. It's a nineteen-twenties, Gothic-style building with huge rooms and twenty-five foot ceilings. For the next couple of weeks we diligently rehearse in one such room.

Watching John direct is profoundly humbling. The man is matchless. Sometimes working the actors like a Beethoven Quartet, other times routing them onto the same path. It's ensemble, exactly the way I wrote it. He's a verifiable genius.

After a few days into the rehearsals, a phone call informs me that John cannot make the rehearsal that day. "So what the hell do I do?" I ask John.

"Salvatore, you wrote the play. Tell them. Show them what you want. Break a leg."

Bink! He hangs up. Ten minutes later, another phone call—this time it's Al Ruscio, he can't make rehearsal either. He's doing a movie with Clint Eastwood. I have a moment of some serious introspection. Should I cancel the rehearsal? I can't, it's too late in the day, actors are on their way there right now. Nope, I gotta do it. What the hell do I know about directing or acting? Shit, I gotta do it. I'm in way the fuck over my head, but I gotta do it. I'm determined to see this play on the boards.

So, an hour later, I'm valiantly attempting to direct and act in the play. The actors are most indulgent, for which I'm utterly grateful. I dutifully plod on. One scene calls for my character (Leonardo) to berate Anthony Caruso's character (Luigi), who is supposed to respond "menacingly." I say my Leonardo line and wait for Luigi's lines. For a moment there is complete silence. Then "Luigi's" eyes slowly narrow into wafer-thin slits, glacial and dark. He stares at me, a deep hard black stare, then unleashes his diatribe, coming down on me like a eighteen-wheeler on a June bug. I'm startled. Jesus, is this guy for real? Doesn't he know that it's just a play? Does he really want to kill me? Is he nuts? I meekly spit out my lines and immediately call for a lunch break. In three seconds, Caruso drops out of character and is laughing and joking with the other actors in the chow line (salami, cheese, bread, olives, sans vino). I learned what acting was all about that day. It's about getting naked and doing a swan dive into a psychological abyss.

After two weeks of rehearsal, I rent the venerable Callboard Theater on Melrose Place, procuring the set, furniture, props, lighting, publicity, etc. Opening night of the play. Full house. I'm beat, all my jump has run out. An hour and forty-five fiercely intense minutes crawl by. Curtain down, it's over. My heart is beating like a bongo drum. Then unanimous applause, a solid affirmation of my writing. Maybe I'm a playwright? Shit, I am a playwright. It feels good. Real fucking good. I'm wearing three hats—writer, producer, and janitor.

Arriving at the theater three hours before curtain time, I set up props, replace burned-out light bulbs, vacuum the theater, scrub the toilets, sweep the steps, clean up the doggie-doo, and do about forty other chores. I'm learning about the theater the hard way. Maybe that's the best way.

Frank de Kova usually shows up an hour before curtain time. He pitches in with cleaning the toilet bowls, sweeping the floors, etc. Invariably he asks me at least ten well thought-out questions about the play and his character. Always searching for nuance and layers of subjectivity, he forces me to think on my feet. This man is an actor right down to his wiggling DNA. He wants to know where I learned dramaturgy. I tell him the same thing I told John—after the run of the play, I shall tell all.

Next, Al Ruscio arrives—Al is an artist, scrupulously well mannered, affable, cheerful. Anthony Caruso is another artist. Always hungry, he first nibbles on the salami and cheese that's used in the play, then changes underwear and puts on a pair of red bikini shorts, reaffirming his character in the play. Then he and Al run lines with each other (reciting dialogue in rapid fire). The rest of the actors—Gloria Manos, John Miranda, Peter Schrum—arrive a half hour before curtain time. Tony Bova usually arrives about three minutes before curtain. I gotta tell ya, this showbiz thing is fraught with anxiety.

We get mixed reviews. Some good, some not so good. I don't know what the hell to make of it. "Salvatore, it doesn't mean a thing. Word of mouth will run this play for weeks," says John. He's right. We're getting bigger audiences each week. However, it's not fast enough. I'm running low on bread, and penniless I do not want to be. After six weeks, I reluctantly close the play. It was one hell of an experience. Enlightening. I've been catapulted into another world. A million miles away from snipping hair.

I tell John Meyhers about my background as a barber. I'm surprised that he wasn't surprised. He assumed that I was either educated at some Eastern university, or was self-educated—saying the best writers are self-educated. He emphasizes to "beware of Hollywood writers" and listen to my own voice, do my own thing. I gotta say, coming from the most brilliant man that I have ever met, it's inspiring.

John throws a party for the cast and crew and a few of his friends. John knows everybody. He's profoundly cultured, quick with wit, quick to laugh. The man is full of energy, his voice sings even when he's speaking. I'm at the party, sitting next to Anthony Caruso, my favorite "bad guy" of the cinema. I was eleven years old the first time I saw his rugged powerful face—it was on a movie screen, his nostrils were as big as canoes. Tony—I call him Tony now—has portrayed mean mobsters, irate Indians, gun-slinging cowboys, the list is long. This man knows Hollywood and its panoply of stars.

Scanning the scene, I see thirty showbiz folk in various stages of inebriation. Tim Conway and Don Knotts are slumping in big easy chairs. I raise my glass of scotch to a toasting position and mime a salute to Tim. He smiles and raises his glass of booze back at me.

An impressive piano glissando slices into the party din and, from a far corner of the room, John's booming voice does just that, booms as he breaks into song from one of his Broadway musicals. After belting out a few tunes, he humbly accepts his applause with a bow and a beaming smile, then gets back to the business of hosting the party.

I'm sitting there thinking of how John had introduced me to everyone as a "brilliant" new playwright. I was stunned. No one has ever introduced me as a playwright before, yet alone as a brilliant one. Right now, I'm not sitting there as a hairdresser, barber, whatever. It's different now. Hey, of course I know that I'm no way near brilliant, but I gotta say, at that moment, I felt absolutely fucking brilliant. I'm part of this whole scene. I'm sharing a place in this room filled with talented showbiz people. Shiiit. Let me ride with this moment, surf the ego wave until it ripples to the mundane shores of reality. See that! I'm starting to sound brilliant already.

I ask Tony, "Been to a lot of parties, Tony?"

"Plenty."

"You know, when I first saw you on screen, your nostrils were as big as canoes."

"So?"

"So nothing. Here I am, years later, beside you. For real."

"Ya thrilled?"

"In a way. Yeah, I'm thrilled."

"It will wear off."

"Man, you've known all the great stars of Hollywood. Robert Taylor."

"We were close friends."

"Jimmy Stewart?"

"Stewart, Mitchum, Cooper, Fonda, Lancaster. Friends. Pretty soon, we'll all be kicking off. Fini."

"It's a bitch, man. We're alive. We're dead. What the fuck is that all about?"

"Allora." (i.e., So it goes.)

"Anyhow. I got to you. Do I look brilliant?"

"How the hell do I know. I'm not that smart."

"Burned."

CHAPTER ELEVEN

A few months down the line, I'm with my friend/agent Peter Meyer at the Century City Hotel. Peter has some legal papers for a client to sign. The client being Sterling Hayden. One of my favorite actors of all time.

At twenty-two, he was a ship's captain. Early in his career, the studio dubbed him "The Most Beautiful Man in the Movies." Later on, he proved himself to be a superior actor in the role of a hoodlum in John Huston's "The Asphalt Jungle." He also made outstanding appearances in Stanley Kubrick's "The Killing" and "Dr. Strangelove," as well as in "Johnny Guitar," "The Godfather," and a string of others. It's a long impressive list. He's also a fine writer. "The Wanderer" and his novel "Voyage" won him critical acclaim. I'm anxious to meet him.

In the elevator on the way up to his room, Peter tells me about a recent experience Sterling had. He landed in jail in Canada for smoking a pipe full of grass while boarding a Canadian airline. His agency (William Morris) got him out of that touchy situation. It seems he doesn't give a hoot about the laws governing marijuana, and believes it's no one's business what he smokes. I don't even know this guy and I like him already.

A couple of discreet knocks on his hotel door. We hear a gravelly "Hold on." We hold...

"He wears a beat-up long robe and sandals and carries a big stick wherever he goes," says Peter.

"Like a Moses thing?" I ask.

"Nah, nothing like that...Well. Maybe."

"What's he into?"

"I dunno. Everything. Did you see him on the Merv Griffin Show last week?"

Before I have a chance to answer, the door cautiously opens and there he is. Man, this guy has been around the block a few dozen times. He's 6'5", barrel-chested, weathered. His wizened boozy face says it all, its cracks and creases a blatant affirmation of a life hard lived. I got a thing about hands. Hands tell all. His hands are massive. We shake, this guy is powerful, I can only imagine his strength when he was a younger man. His room is a modest one-bedroom number. First thing I notice is a big mound of rumpled clothing in the center of an unused bed. Bam! Sterling picks up my thoughts.

"I never sleep on a bed," he says to me in a raspy voice.

"Where's your stick?" Peter asks Sterling.

"It's a staff. I lost it, man," he fretfully mutters.

"Do you remember where?" Peter continues.

"No. Too much wine. I miss that staff."

I can't help it, it's an optimum moment to work my Zen chops.

"You lost the staff. Someone will find it. Perfect. Exactly as it should be. Call it 'The Transmission of The Staff,'" I shamelessly spout with a voice louder than I had intended.

There's a long beat while Sterling looks at me. Fortunately, it's a benign look. "God bless you, man," he says in a chummy voice, "A sip of wine?"

Peter declines, I accept. We sit down. Peter gets right to business, has Sterling sign the movie contracts. Fifteen minutes later, Peter's ready to leave. I stay. Peter splits.

"Care for some smoke?" asks Sterling.

"Absolutely," I promptly reply.

Sterling goes into his bedroom. In a few seconds, he returns carrying a burnished sea chest, which he gingerly places before me. Then slowly and reverently, he opens the chest. I catch a glimpse of a few rumpled photos, eating utensils, a couple of wineglasses, and a huge 18th century smoking pipe. He digs deeper into the chest and emerges with a baggy full of primo weed. Ceremoniously filling the pipe bowl with the weed, he dives back into the chest, comes up with a box of wooden matches. Striking a match on the sole of his sandal, he carefully lights the pipe, has a capacious hit, holds it, then gently hands the pipe to me.

Several whacko hours later, what with cheap wine (he likes the sugary Muscatel), weed, and blow (I had a taste with me), we were having a hell of a good time. Talking all kinds of stuff. Zen, mysticism, art, movies, sailing, the sea, writing, acting. Sterling hates acting, says he's a lousy actor and only does it for the money. Once in awhile the phone would ring and he would reluctantly answer. He'd politely listen for about thirty seconds, then, in his basso-profondo voice, say "Goodbye and God bless you, man" and abruptly hang up.

"Actors," he wheezes to me referring to the phone call. "Fucked-up bunch. 'Eh, man?"

"We're all fucked up," I unconsciously add.

"True. God bless you, man."

"At least the Italians have style."

Now he goes into a stream-of-thought thing, about the time he lived in Italy, the Italian people, the culture, the style. He veers into France, lays out the French trip for me...then Germany, Ireland, etc. Four o'clock in the morning, we've been all over the globe. I'm wiped out, hanging. I crawl home.

That's how it goes for the next couple of weeks. I visit Sterling in his hotel room, we get fucked up, we rap. So we're into some heavy shit about—shit, I forgot what the hell is was about, but it was heavy. All of a sudden, Sterling rises from the floor on which he's been squatting, slides open the sliding doors and steps out onto the balcony. He takes a deep breath and, holding an imaginary bow, turns his back to the sun. Then from an imaginary quiver, he notches an imaginary arrow, turns and faces the day's sun slowly dropping from the horizon. He expertly draws the bow like Robin Hood, takes aim at the center of the sinking orange-bright sun. The seconds crawl by...Sterling, still as alabaster, holds his aim...the sun imperceptibly sinking...then Sterling shoots his arrow. Zip! Bink! The sun is gone.

That over, Sterling closes the balcony doors and squats himself back on the floor. "We made it through another day, man...One more day gone," he says to himself.

Several hours later, we're rolling along nicely on another trippy-rap, when we hear a couple of taps on the door. We both stop in mid-rap, look blankly at each other.

"You order something, man?" I ask.

"Don't think so."

There are a couple more discreet taps on the door. Sterling uncurls himself from the floor, wobbles to his feet, goes to the door and squints through the peephole. "Shit. I forgot. It's the cab driver. Well. Good. Good." Sterling opens the door. "Come in, my good man. God bless you. Come in."

The cabbie meekly eases his way into the room. He looks to be East Indian. Now, looking at Sterling, he stifles a surprised breath.

"You an actor?" he blurts.

"Sometimes, my good man," says Sterling.

"You call for cab?" the cabbie asks.

"Yes, yes. I did. God bless you, man."

"Where to?"

"San Francisco."

"San Francisco?"

"Yes, my good man. Sit down, have a drink or smoke or both, whatever. God bless you, man. Are you a good driver?"

"Very good, sir," replies the cabbie verily.

"Good. Good. God bless you, man."

That's the last time I saw Sterling, motoring to San Francisco with a very stoned cabdriver. Sterling died of a heart attack a year later. He was sixty-four years old. Trippy guy...

Onward a couple of lean years. I've been gleaning a modest living writing kid's animated cartoons for TV, plus selling a few options on my screenplays. I figure my ken is playwriting. I've written a few more, like I don't really give a damn if they're produced. No, that's not it. I give a damn—I'm burning to get on the boards with the plays—it's just that I don't want to go through all the Hollywood bullshit to make it happen. In screenwriting, everybody pokes their omniscient nose into your screenplay, sniffing and snorting, then ripping it into shreds like irate pit bulls. That doesn't happen with playwriting. In playwriting, the playwright has control of the work. That will probably get fucked up too.

An unexpected phone call from John Meyhers. He says he's been directing plays at a little theater in the Valley. One of the plays he was to direct has been cancelled. That leaves an opening to slip in my latest play. I titled it "Is Anyone Else In The Dream?" It's a comedy about agoraphobia. John figures he can convince the producer to do it. Am I interested? Does a cat have fur balls? Hell yes, I'm interested.

I'm pumped and ready to roll. The whole scene is in double time. We quickly have an audition for actors, followed by eight quick days of rehearsal, followed by an unpublicized opening. I'm seriously ambivalent about the production. The play is "there," or rather shadows of the play are there. John's directing is nimble as ever, still?

Okay, it needs more work—and the actors are scrupulously mediocre, save one, Herb Graham, who plays a Viennese psychiatrist, he's super. Maybe I should have waited until I nailed some really good actors and had a little more time for rehearsal? Still, I got the work produced. So the production was not the greatest. Next time, it will be better. Now the good part—the play is getting damn nice reviews, and I'm now a legit card-carrying Dramatist! Feels good.

Let's jump ahead ten years. I'm with my lady, Mary Karacus. She's a universe onto herself. Unequivocally, the most honest, straightforward person I have ever known. I love her. That feels good too. Right now I'm kicked back on my sofa, scrolling my memory banks, thinking about the Memphis Mafia—"the Guys."

When the unflattering book "Elvis, What Happened?" was published (ironically in the same month that Elvis died), it publicly detailed for the first time the reality of Elvis' private world by those who had been closest to him. Elvis was devastated by what he saw as Red and Sonny West's betrayal of their friendship by their "tattletaling." Tense times do not call for the usual celebrity bowing, and when Elvis wanted straight answers, he got them from Li'l Billy, who Elvis knew he could trust. Li'l Billy turned out to be a for-real person. When I knew him, he was an ass-kisser, like the rest of the Guys (except for Joe Esposito), but it was Li'l Billy who stuck by Elvis when everyone else was jumping ship.

Elvis found a centering for his life with his bug-eyed cousin Billy, who certified his country roots and took him back to his once callow innocence. Billy stuck with Elvis all the way. I haven't seen him for years, however, I've learned that he's turned into a mature and bright guy. Hooray for Billy!

The rest of the guys? Alan Fortis died of a heart attack. Jim Kingsley committed suicide. Richard "The Broom," last I heard he was a security guard at a Reno casino. Sonny West, my man, has been writing screenplays. Marty Laker became a record producer. Jerry Schilling is a top honcho for "Elvis Presley Enterprises." Red West is now a drama teacher and actor—and a damn good actor. "Diamond Joe" Esposito, well, I'm not sure. Right now, scratching my grey beard, I'm realizing that I miss the sing-song, quick-as-a-wink repartee from the Guys, the colorful asperities, the "down to the sod" aphorisms. I get a good feeling thinking about them, like a kitten pressing against a warm brick.

I'm half watching TV. The program is about haunted houses and mysterious deaths, spooky stuff. H.A. Benza is the host and narrator of the show. He's talking about a mysterious house, a jinxed house, and how the people who have lived in the jinxed house have had tragic and mysterious deaths. Now he mentions that Jean Harlow's lover, Paul Berns, committed suicide in the house. Now H.A. has my full attention. I kick up the volume. H.A. goes on to say how the house is jinxed. The same house, Jay's house, where Jay and I were instructed by Bruce Lee— where I had super dinners with Jay and Sharon Tate. The house where Jay informed me about doing Elvis' hair...

Friends...Gone. Jay Sebring, he wanted to be famous, he is, for the Charlie Manson murders.

Friends—Gone. Elvis. Gone...What a fucking waste...

Life moves in unavailing circles, then you reach the end of your career, you've made your "goal," then it's time to look at the other side of it. Time for serious questions as you consider the scenes of your life story. Time for truth and candor.

I'm standing in front of my Laurel Canyon love-cottage. The street is quiet and chilly. It's the same—as if I had never been away. I have no idea who lives there now. The backyard. My backyard. I slept in the sun there. I dreamed and built a world for myself there. I hear Marilyn's infectious giggle. I'm crying.

Looking back on the whole scene. The show, the dough, the woe. The era. Errors. The fun, the sun, the romance, the famous. The movement of my legs carrying me across the misty sands of life. The gift of precious years in a world where anguish was so much less than it is today. The rain, the feel of beach sand beneath my feet, and a rolling ocean whispering its eternal song.

Made in the USA
San Bernardino, CA
23 February 2017